Introduction

The southern beautiful wa ____ ____ills of northeast ____ ____ouded peaks of the Great Smoky Mount. ___, nundreds of these scenic natural wonders are located throughout the region. Everything from tiny, intricate cascades to thundering cataracts - a tremendous variety of falling water makes its home in Blue Ridge country.

The majority of the waterfalls in the southern Appalachians occur on relatively small streams with drops which could generally be classified as minor to moderate. Occasionally you'll find a major drop along a moderately-sized creek or small river. Examples of these would be the waterfalls in the escarpment region of North and South Carolina such as Whitewater Falls or the falls on the Cullasaja River between Highlands and Franklin, North Carolina. Other notable major falls occur in several of the spectacular gorges of the southern Appalachians such as Tallulah Gorge in northeast Georgia or Linville Gorge in North Carolina.

While a few of the waterfalls in this book are somewhat isolated from other cascades, waterfalls often occur in clusters which allow enthusiasts to visit several in a short amount of time. Examples of this are several of the northeast Georgia or western North Carolina "hubs" that feature as many as 10-12 waterfalls in a fairly concentrated area.

I have broken this guidebook into several distinct areas. First, the waterfalls are organized by state (with the exception being that I included the cascades of the Great Smoky Mountains National Park, both TN and NC, into one section). I have then organized the waterfalls into logical geographical hubs that would allow visitors to maximize their time. In several cases, such as the falls in Rabun County, GA, waterfalls in more than one hub could be easily accessed from the same general area. Refer to the state or regional maps in the book for a general overview, then refer to the individual hub maps to organize your visits.

I would like to make one point quite clear from the start. This publication is not meant to be a definitive comprehensive collection of southern Appalachian waterfalls. Each waterfall in this guidebook has been personally selected from a larger list of falls in the region. For the most part I have tried to feature waterfalls that can be reached via relatively short, easy to moderate hikes. Many of the waterfalls in this book are accessed by trails shorter than one mile.

I've also tried to stay away from many of the waterfalls that are difficult to find and/or dangerous to access. Every now and then I've found myself including a few cascades that have no maintained trail because they are simply too beautiful to pass up. In this case I have tried to emphasize both the challenges and the dangers. Ultimately however, the responsibility lies with each individual visitor as to whether or not you should attempt to visit a particular waterfall. Nearly all of the waterfalls are either on National Forest land or within the boundaries of state parks. There are a few waterfalls in this guidebook which are on private property; they are either visible from a public road or the owners allow visitors to come onto their property to view them.

I've also tried to include a large *variety* of falling water. Several other excellent waterfall guidebooks vary somewhat in their interpretation of a particular cascade's beauty. I too have my favorites but realized long ago that my "taste" in waterfalls was way too subjective. In this guidebook I give a very general rating from "fair" to "good" to "excellent" to "spectacular" and you may certainly disagree with my ratings. I've chosen four broad categories because a waterfall's beauty at any given time depends on a number of factors including stream flow, time of day, season and the number of visitors present. No doubt the biggest variable is a person's personal preference.

One thing is certain - this book will keep getting bigger and bigger. Since the first 64 page edition in 1990, *Waterfalls of the Southern Appalachians* continues to grow. Every time I update an edition it ends up growing by a dozen or more waterfalls. The geographical area covered by the book is growing as well, extending further northeast into the North Carolina mountains as well as west toward the ridge and valley sections of Georgia and Tennessee. It's a bit of a lifelong obsession I suppose.

Whatever *your* preference, it is my hope that this book will help you discover these gems of God's creation. I have attempted to supply accurate descriptions, directions, maps and photos in order to make your waterfall explorations easier, safer, and more enjoyable. Be safe - I hope to see you on the trail.

Sincerely,

Brian

Waterfall Descriptions

Realizing that most people who obtain a guidebook are looking for simple descriptions and accurate directions, I have tried to keep things short and sweet. For each waterfall there are a few basics provided just beneath the name. For example:

Stream: Amicalola Creek   USGS Quad: Nimblewill, GA
Rating: excellent   Landowner: Amicalola Falls State Park
Type: free-falling/cascade   Trail length: approx. 0.25 mile (one way)
Height: 729 feet   Difficulty: moderate, paved with steps
Stream flow: medium   Elevation: 1,900 feet

As mentioned in the introduction, ratings are quite subjective. I have attempted to generalize these into four categories: fair, good, excellent and spectacular. Any waterfall rated as excellent or spectacular is a *must-see*. As far as type, waterfalls are (generally) either free-falling, a cascade or a waterslide. Most are a combination of two or even all three.

The height category is the measurement from the brink (top) of the waterfall to the base. Many of the waterfalls in this guidebook have been carefully measured and their heights meticulously documented. However, some of the waterfalls are listed with heights that are merely estimated.

Stream flow is another fairly general classification. Those listed as small are generally creeks or brooks. Waterfalls along these streams are drastically affected by drought and the resulting low water conditions. Those classified as large are generally large creeks or rivers which will under normal conditions feature a respectable flow year round.

Trail lengths are provided as one way distances. These figures are generally provided in yards when the distance is fairly small or in tenths of a mile. The difficulty ratings are also quite subjective depending on age and physical condition of the visitor. An "easy" rating means just about anyone should be able to visit the waterfall. "Moderate" normally means that there will be a few challenges. This could relate to distance, elevation change (including steps) or other challenging or dangerous conditions. "Difficult" or "strenuous" may also be used to describe the trail. I have tried to be specific as to the challenges or dangers whenever these terms are used.

I have also attempted to provide USGS Quadrangle information whenever possible. This information was gleaned from maps, other publications or from internet sources. Above all I've tried to keep it simple.

Trail Hazards

It's great to think that every hike into waterfall country will turn out fine, but there are a few items worth mentioning to keep you on your toes. By all means enjoy your hike and all the great scenery, but always be aware of your surroundings. For many hikers poison ivy is enemy #1 in the great outdoors. From April through November you run a good chance of brushing up against this irritating (literally) vine. If you will familiarize yourself with its trademark grouping of three leaves you can probably avoid the resulting miserable experience.

Many varieties of snakes make their homes in the woods and streams of the Blue Ridge. While your chances of seeing a poisonous variety are fairly slim, at least two types are fairly common throughout the region. Copperheads and timber rattlesnakes can be found just about anywhere. Be on guard particularly if you are venturing through heavy brush or stepping over an obstacle such as a downed tree. In the span of two weeks in the summer of 2009 I came across an adult copperhead (North Rim Trail - Tallulah Gorge State Park) and a *very impressive* (i.e. terrifying) adult timber rattler (Cohutta Wilderness - Beech Bottom Trail), both parked right in the middle of the trail. Usually if you back off and make a commotion they will gladly yield the trail to you.

Wasps and yellow jackets are another common hazard in the great outdoors. Yellow jackets love to nest in the ground, particularly in the wood of rotting stumps or roots. Be aware of where you step at all times. Hornets and wasps often make enormous grey-paper nests that hang from the limbs of trees.

In the summer of 2009, while climbing down to the plunge pool at the waterfall on Little Rock Creek near Suches, I grabbed the limb of a rhododendron tree and was immediately swarmed by hundreds of white-faced hornets who had made a well-camouflaged nest in the lower limbs of the tree. In the eternity of the minute or so that followed I was stung approximately 40 times from head to ankles. In the furious scramble to make my escape I fell several times tearing a rotator cuff and severely spraining an ankle. The hornets finally gave up as I thrashed about in the waterfall's shallow plunge pool. Luckily I was able to hike nearly a mile back to my vehicle. I now carry an epi-pen just in case I have an allergic reaction to a bee sting. Though not always possible try to hike with someone when you can, and *always let someone know where you are*. Your greatest hazard may well be the other humans in the woods at any given time. Use caution and good common sense when in the wild.

Waterfall Safety Tips

There are a few simple rules that may keep you from serious harm or even death when visiting a waterfall:

- *Do not climb on waterfalls.* Many people have died doing this.
- *Always view a waterfall from the base*; try to avoid the brink of the falls - it is very slippery! The view is best from the base anyway.
- *Do not cross a stream above a waterfall.* There have been numerous deaths around the country from people falling into streams and being swept to their deaths over waterfalls. Any stream crossing regardless of location can be hazardous. It only takes a few inches of moving water to knock over an adult. If your foot becomes lodged between rocks the force of the current can hold you underwater. Many people drown on fast moving rivers this way.
- *Utilize observation platforms.* It's always tempting to try and get a bit closer, but streams and streamside rocks can be treacherously slippery. It also helps protect the fragile streamside environment.

You may witness stupidity in an ultimate form while visiting the waterfalls in this book. People are all too eager to disregard their safety for a closer look or a bit of fun. Be safe and use good common sense.

Best Times to Visit Waterfall Country

Everyone always asks - when is the best time to view waterfalls? Quite simply - anytime the water levels are high, or as the old saying goes, "your best bet is when its wet." The wetter months of winter and spring usually feature the highest stream levels. These months also offer the advantages of more comfortable temperatures, no leaves to obscure your view, lack of insects and snakes, and far fewer fellow humans to compete with.

I personally love each and every season, but it's hard to do better than a temperate late fall or winter day basking on a streamside rock and enjoying a waterfall at full flow. Autumn is a spectacular time in the southern Blue Ridge but all too often the waterfalls of the region are at their yearly low flows. In the summer months I always try to get out and visit my favorite waterfalls immediately after a few days of moderate to heavy rain when the vegetation is green and lush and the waterfalls are freshly rejuvenated. As a rule, I tend to avoid falls on the smaller streams in late summer or fall as they tend to greatly diminish.

Waterfall Photography

When it comes to photography, I'm a self-professed "hacker." I love to photograph waterfalls but I am largely untrained and have learned from experience. What I do know however, is that if you experiment and take a lot of photos the odds are better that you'll get something you like. In this day and age of high quality digital cameras, there's really no reason why you can't become an accomplished waterfall photographer. Briefly, here are Boyd's rules for the novice photographer:

- *Use a tripod.* The only way to create the "blurred water" effect is to use a slow shutter speed, and the only way to steady your camera in order to do this is with a tripod. Hint: lightweight is good.
- *Shutter speed.* If shooting in full sun conditions and you want to "freeze" the falling water, a fast shutter speed (1/500 +) will give you good results. For the blurred water effect described above, you'll need to slow way down. I like to shoot anywhere from 1/10 second to 1 second exposures, and will often experiment with as many as 40-50 exposures at a single waterfall.
- *Lighting conditions.* Even lighting is always best but rarely do you meet with perfect conditions. You can usually find nice even lighting around dawn, dusk, and on overcast days. If you try to shoot a waterfall in half sun, half shade you'll rarely get good results.
- *Depth of field.* This refers to the portions of your photo that are in sharp focus. If you have good foreground items that you want included in your shot, you should set your camera to the aperture mode and choose a high number (f 22, etc). If you want a narrow depth of field with only the prime subject in focus, select a low number and carefully focus on the prime subject.
- *Stay composed.* Not you personally, just your photo. Try to place an interesting object in the foreground (a rock, flower, etc.). Also become familiar with the "rule of thirds" and try to offset your primary target in the photograph. One simple technique is to imagine a tic-tac-toe grid on your camera screen and place key components of your shot on one of the line intersections.
- *Get a good book or research the topic on the internet.* While these tips will get you going, there's no substitute for good research and there are literally dozens of articles on the internet alone that will teach you good technique for shooting waterfalls.

Table of Contents

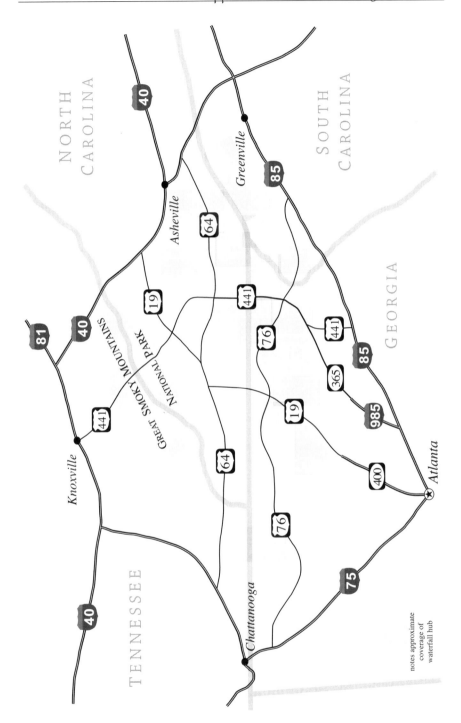

notes approximate
coverage of
waterfall hub

Waterfalls of the Southern Appalachians and Great Smoky Mountains

To my father,

Lawrence Boyd,

who passed away December 29, 2010.
I enjoyed our many hikes over the years.
Thank you for your faithfulness and
for always setting the right example.

Section I

northeast
Georgia

Georgia Hub #1 - Dahlonega

Historic Dahlonega is the site of the first major gold strike in the United States. In 1828, over two decades before the great 1849 gold rush in California, gold was being pulled out of the red clay hills of North Georgia. So much gold, in fact, that the U.S. Mint operated a branch here from 1838-1861. Gold is so symbolic in these parts that the steep spire of Price Memorial Hall on the campus of North Georgia College and State University is layered in gold. For a detailed history be sure to visit the Dahlonega Gold Museum in the old courthouse building in the middle of town square.

Dahlonega is one of Georgia's quintessential mountain towns. In fact, it may be the closest "mountain town" to the city. If you want to get out of the city and into the mountains fast, just head up Georgia 400 and you'll be there in a bit over an hour (depending on Atlanta traffic, of course). Dahlonega offers one of the nicest town squares you'll ever visit with dozens of interesting shoppes and restaurants. It's also the home of several excellent festivals such as Gold Rush Days in the fall.

There are many excellent waterfalls in the area but some involve long and difficult hikes; others are wilderness waterfalls which are inherently dangerous. I've included two excellent waterfalls that require relatively little effort to view. Amicalola Falls is one of Georgia's most well known and it's about 20 miles west of town. The other, Cane Creek Falls, is on the grounds of nearby Camp Glisson who currently allows visitors to view the waterfall as long as they don't have camp in session.

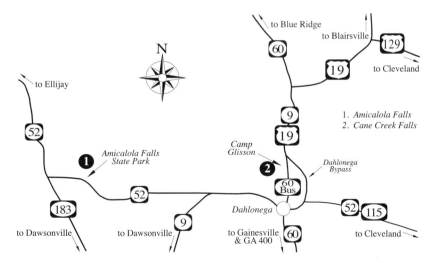

Amicalola Falls ★

Stream: Amicalola Creek
Rating: excellent
Type: free-falling/cascade
Height: 200 feet upper cascades
Stream flow: medium

USGS Quad: Nimblewill, GA
Landowner: Amicalola Falls State Park
Trail length: approx. 0.25 mile (one way)
Difficulty: moderate, paved with steps
Elevation: 1,900 feet

Amicalola Falls
upper cascades

Directions

Amicalola Falls State Park is located on GA. 52 approximately 18 miles west of Dahlonega, 15 miles north of Dawsonville, and 19 miles southeast of Ellijay. The trailhead is located at the far end of the park entrance road alongside a large reflection pool. Entrance fees are required.

Trail and description

Amicalola is generally believed to be derived from the Cherokee word for *tumbling waters*. If true this is one waterfall that lives up to its name. At 729 feet this waterfall is "officially" listed as Georgia's highest, but only the upper several hundred feet are readily visible. The lower two-thirds consist of a prolonged series of steep cascades which, though within earshot, are tough to view. A scenic pool at the trailhead once offered a beautiful vista of the waterfall, but over time the forest canopy has grown to the point where the waterfall is difficult to view except in the leafless months of late fall to early spring. Because this portion of the stream is in a fairly small watershed the personality of the falls can change drastically along with the stream flow. Amicalola casts a particularly inviting spell during the high runoff periods of winter and early spring. Be aware that Amicalola Falls State Park is one of Georgia's most popular state parks. It not only possesses great scenery but is the starting point for the 7-mile Appalachian Trail approach path. The best view of the cascade is generally from the bridge spanning the creek just below the upper cascades. There are other good vantage points along the upper portion of the trail as well, but be advised: the somewhat short walk from the parking area is quite steep and involves a heart-pumping series of switchbacks and stairs.

Cane Creek Falls ★

Stream: Cane Creek
Rating: excellent
Type: steep cascade
Height: 30 feet
Stream flow: medium

USGS Quad: Dahlonega, GA
Landowner: Camp Glisson (private)
Trail length: short walk
Difficulty: easy
Elevation: 1,220 feet

Cane Creek Falls

Directions
        From downtown Dahlonega follow Hwy. 60 Business north for 2 miles. Turn left onto Cane Creek Road. Proceed 0.8 miles to the camp welcome center. Park and obtain permission to view the falls. Note the camp may be closed to the public during camps, conferences, and retreats.

Description
        There are a lot of things to like about this waterfall, *if* you can plan your visit appropriately. The beautiful 30-foot cascade is located on the grounds of Camp Glisson, a United Methodist facility. Once you obtain

permission walk downhill along the road to an observation deck at the brink of this surprisingly powerful waterfall. Several good photo vantage points are located along the stream bank just downstream of the waterfall as well.

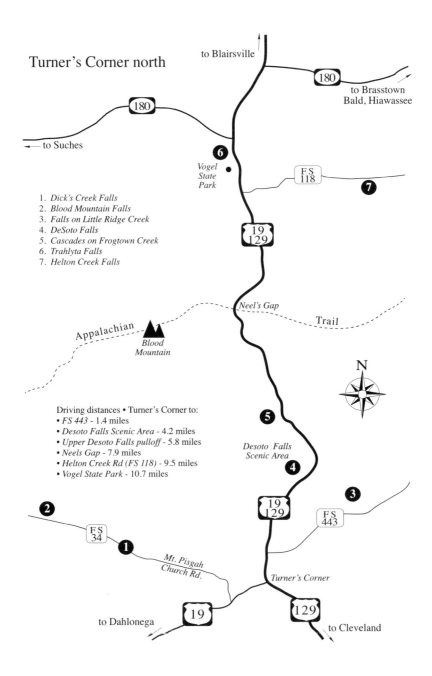

Turner's Corner north

to Blairsville

180

to Brasstown
Bald, Hiawassee

180

to Suches

6

Vogel
State
Park

F S
118

7

1. *Dick's Creek Falls*
2. *Blood Mountain Falls*
3. *Falls on Little Ridge Creek*
4. *DeSoto Falls*
5. *Cascades on Frogtown Creek*
6. *Trahlyta Falls*
7. *Helton Creek Falls*

19
129

Neel's Gap

Trail

Appalachian

Blood
Mountain

N

Driving distances • Turner's Corner to:
• *FS 443* - 1.4 miles
• *Desoto Falls Scenic Area* - 4.2 miles
• *Upper Desoto Falls pulloff* - 5.8 miles
• *Neels Gap* - 7.9 miles
• *Helton Creek Rd (FS 118)* - 9.5 miles
• *Vogel State Park* - 10.7 miles

5

*Desoto Falls
Scenic Area*

4

3

2

F S
34

1

19
129

F S
443

*Mt. Pisgah
Church Rd.*

Turner's Corner

to Dahlonega

19

129

to Cleveland

Georgia Hub #2 - Turner's Corner to Vogel

Overview

The scenic drive from Turner's Corner to Blairsville is through the very heart of the beautiful North Georgia Mountains. This dramatic route takes visitors past the lush DeSoto Falls Scenic area and ascends the rugged southern flank of lofty Blood Mountain past historic Neel's Gap and the legendary Appalachian Trail. From here a heart-pounding 1,400-foot ascent carries hikers to the top of Blood Mountain, the highest point on the AT in Georgia. To the north Highway 19/129 begins a long descent past popular Vogel State Park to the upper reaches of the Nottely River watershed. The Nottely flows north toward the bustling tourist-friendly village of Blairsville, home to a number of seasonal fairs and events. Georgia Highway 180 heads west just north of Vogel State Park toward the beautiful Winfield Scott Scenic Area, while 180 east climbs to the spectacular summit of 4,784-foot Brasstown Bald, the tallest peak in Georgia. Oh, and by the way, there are some great waterfalls here as well.

Dick's Creek Falls

Stream: Waters Creek   USGS Quad: Neel's Gap, GA
Rating: excellent   Landowner: Chattahoochee National Forest
Type: steep cascade   Trail length: short walk
Height: 12 feet   Difficulty: easy
Stream flow: large   Elevation: 1,740 feet

Dick's Creek Falls

Directions

From Turner's Corner follow Hwy. 19 south toward Dahlonega for 0.5 mile. Turn left onto Mt. Pisgah Church Road and drive 2.6 miles to the parking area on the right. The waterfall is just across the road down the well worn path.

Description

Dick's Creek Falls is located just below the confluence of Dick's Creek and Waters Creek. All the elements of a great waterfall come together here as this broad, rocky cascade is bordered by deep green laurel and hemlock. The water volume is normally adequate enough to create a nice photo in nearly any season. A sloped shelf of slippery rocks extends down to the creek on the approach side and the dark green plunge pool below the cascade is one of the prettiest in the Georgia mountains. The waterfall is perhaps best photographed from several hundred feet downstream, and several locations are accessible just below the road. Dick's Creek Falls is a popular swimming hole and becomes extremely crowded (and a bit trashy) during the warm summer months. A series of rugged cascades is just upstream of the waterfall and is worth exploring as well.

Falls on Blood Mountain Creek

Stream: Blood Mountain Creek
Rating: good
Type: steep cascades
Height: 15 feet
Stream flow: small

USGS Quad: Neel's Gap, GA
Landowner: Blood Mountain Wilderness
Trail length: 150 yards
Difficulty: moderate - not for children
Elevation: 1,980 feet

Directions

From Turner's Corner follow Hwy. 19 south toward Dahlonega for 0.5 mile. Turn left onto Mt. Pisgah Church Road (which becomes FS 34) and drive 4.5 miles to the point where Blood Mountain Creek crosses the road over a culvert/low water bridge. Cross and park on the opposite side (DO NOT attempt to cross this ford if the creek is high!)

Trail and description

A well worn primitive path heads upstream along the left side of the creek. Generally it is easier to take the higher of the paths, then descend to creek level. About 100 yards up the path is a cascade known as lower falls. It plunges through a cleft in the rocks into a narrow pool hemmed in by imposing rock walls which slope steeply to the edge of the creek.

About 75 yards further upstream is another scenic cascade which is set among a scattering of large boulders. There are other smaller cascades even further upstream, but reaching them requires some serious scrambling along steep, slippery terrain. The two lower falls are by far the most scenic along this portion of the creek.

Falls on Little Ridge Creek

Stream: Little Ridge Creek
Rating: good
Type: steep cascades
Height: 15 - 25 feet
Stream flow: small

USGS Quad: Neel's Gap, GA
Landowner: Chestatee WMA
Trail length: 0.6 mile (one way)
Difficulty: moderate - not for children
Elevation: 2,040 feet

Directions

From Turner's Corner follow Hwy. 19 north for 1.4 miles and turn right onto FS 443. Proceed 2 miles to a point where the road fords the creek. Park here. The trail begins to the left beyond the vehicle-blocking mounds.

Trail and description

Backcountry waterfalls require a bit of work but are nearly always free of crowds. The falls on Little Ridge Creek are a perfect example. Follow an old logging road upstream along the creek. At 0.4 mile, about 100 yards beyond the third small branch you step across, proceed along a primitive path to the right to the edge of the creek and find a suitable crossing point. Once across, ascend uphill to an old logging road and follow it upstream as it parallels the creek. The creek is usually not in sight of the road but is normally within earshot. After about 0.1 mile look for a primitive path that drops to the base of the lower cascade. Two other cascades are upstream, spaced about 100 yards apart. Scramble paths lead down to the most popular viewing points of each cascade. Use extreme caution as the approach paths are steep and slippery.

*Little Ridge Creek
lower cascade*

Desoto Falls

Stream: Frogtown Creek tributaries
Rating:upper: good; lower: fair
Type: cascades
Height: upper 80 feet
Stream flow: small

USGS Quad: Neel's Gap, GA
Landowner: Desoto Falls Scenic Area
Trail length: 0.7 mile (one way)
Difficulty: easy to moderate
Elevation: 2,000 feet

Directions

From Turner's Corner follow Hwy. 19 north for 4.2 miles. Turn left into the Desoto Falls Scenic Area and park. There is a nominal charge for day use here. Follow the path through the camping area for several hundred yards to the footbridge over splashing Frogtown Creek. The trail begins here.

Trail and description

Though the curiously named cascades found here are not the most well-known in the region, they are still worth a look. A visitor could easily walk to both waterfalls in about an hour, and the forest scenery alone is worth the visit. The path begins at the wooden footbridge spanning tumbling Frogtown Creek. The larger of the falls is upper falls, about 0.7 mile along the trail to the right. The path crosses the upper falls tributary creek just before turning left and accessing the base of the drop. This pretty 80-foot cascade tumbles in roller coaster fashion over four distinct ledges. A nice observation platform at the base provides a safe vantage point to view the pretty cascade.

*the lower cascades
of upper Desoto falls*

A keen eye will reveal that the trail once extended beyond this point. At one time the path continued to yet another waterfall farther upstream on Frogtown Creek. In other words, the cascade now known as upper falls was once middle falls. It can be confusing if your literature is not up to date. Retrace your route back to the trailhead footbridge and continue along the main path in the opposite direction for several hundred yards, climbing somewhat along a short loop trail up to a viewing platform to lower falls. This splashing 25-foot cascade occurs along a tiny tributary creek and virtually disappears during prolonged dry spells.

Side note

The area is named for the Spanish explorer Hernando Desoto who reportedly passed through the northeast Georgia mountains in the 1500s looking for gold and treasure. Legend has it that early settlers in the area found a mysterious piece of Spanish armor and attributed it to Desoto and his men.

Cascades on Upper Frogtown Creek

Stream: Frogtown Creek   USGS Quad: Neel's Gap, GA
Rating: good   Landowner: Chattahoochee Natl. Forest
Type: slides and steep cascades   Trail length: roadside
Stream flow: small   Difficulty: n/a
Height: 40 feet   Elevation: Approx. 2,200 feet

Directions

From Turner's Corner follow Hwy. 19 north for 5.8 miles (1.6 miles north of Desoto Falls Scenic Area) to a roadside pull-off.

Description

A series of cascades along upper Frogtown Creek is visible from a roadside pull-off along Hwy. 19/129. The cascades will be off to your left as you head north toward Neel's Gap. These cascades are easily visible in the distant ravine in the leafless months of late fall through early spring. Use extreme caution along this busy portion of the highway. The combination of distracting scenery, hairpin curves and impatient drivers can create a dangerous situation.

Trahlyta Falls

Stream: Wolf Creek	USGS Quad: Coosa Bald, GA
Rating: excellent	Landowner: Vogel State Park
Type: cascade	Trail length: 1 mile loop
Height: 40-feet	Difficulty: easy
Stream flow: small	Elevation: approx. 2,600 feet

Directions

From Turner's Corner follow Hwy. 19 north for approximately 11 miles. Turn left into Vogel State Park and proceed to the visitors center. The trail begins at the footbridge over Wolf Creek.

Trail and description

Beautiful Vogel State Park is one of Georgia's two original state parks and is still considered one of the best. Since 1931 visitors have enjoyed camping, hiking, fishing, pedal-boating and swimming in the beautiful 233-acre park. Vogel is a mandatory destination if you're traveling through this portion of North Georgia. A one mile loop trail circles beautiful Lake Trahlyta, named for a famed Cherokee princess. This hike offers a tremendous variety of great scenery. At the western end of the loop atop the lake's earthen dam the 200-yard long Falls Bottom Trail descends to an observation point overlooking the rushing 40-foot cascade and its signature black ledges.

The observation deck is positioned in somewhat of an unusual location near the base of the cascade. From this position you are so close to the falls that photographs will capture only a portion of the cascade. To get a look at the entire waterfall, exit the park and drive north for 0.1 mile. Park on the west side of the highway in the large pull-off.

Trahlyta Falls
upper cascades

Helton Creek Falls ★

Stream: Helton Creek
Rating: excellent
Type: steep waterslide
Height: Upper falls - 60 feet
Stream flow: medium

USGS Quad: Coosa Bald, GA
Landowner: Chattahoochee National Forest
Trail length: 150 yards (one way)
Difficulty: easy (some steps)
Elevation: 2,150 feet

Directions

From Turner's Corner follow Hwy. 19 north for approximately 9.5 miles (approximately 11 miles south of Blairsville). Turn right onto Helton Creek Road (which becomes FS 118) and drive 2.3 miles to a small parking area on the right. The first .7 mile is paved; after that the road is narrow and bumpy in spots.

Helton Creek Falls

Trail and description

Helton Creek Falls is a beautiful cascade just a short drive from Vogel State Park. This waterfall actually features two delightfully different cascades separated by just a few hundred feet. From the parking area walk several hundred feet to a side trail on the left which leads out to a granite shelf near the base of the tumbling 30-foot lower cascade. This waterfall is very scenic but be very careful as the spray soaked rocks can be quite slippery.

Return to the main trail and climb a short series of steps that lead up to a nice observation deck overlooking the main attraction - beautiful upper Helton Creek Falls and its emerald-green boulder-studded plunge pool. The cascade is perfectly framed against a cliff of grey rock. The waterfall is particularly impressive during periods of high water when it seems to fill the cliff face. Because it occurs high in the Helton Creek watershed it can diminish greatly during dry spells. It is however a great waterfall to visit regardless of the season: autumn frames the cascade with a vivid display of colorful leaves; in winter ice forms across the face of the cliff; in spring and summer wildflowers and rhododendrons bloom.

Not too many years ago this cascade received only light visitation but as word has gotten around the crowds have discovered Helton Creek Falls. Try to plan your visit on a weekday during the summer months. Early mornings are a particularly good time to visit this charming waterfall.

Georgia Hub #3 - Suches

Scenic Georgia Highway 60 cuts a swath through one of the most undeveloped portions of North Georgia. From Dahlonega the highway rises along a series of seemingly never-ending curves before reaching the Appalachian Trail at Woody Gap, then descends into the sleepy hamlet of Suches. North of Suches GA 60 provides access into the beautiful 1240-acre Cooper Creek Scenic Area, a favorite of north Georgia hikers.

Highway 60 closely follows the beautiful Toccoa River for several miles between Suches and Morganton. Deep Hole Recreation Area is conveniently located on Hwy. 60 along the banks of the scenic stream. Camping and trout fishing are the main attractions here. Another popular destination in the area is the Chattahoochee Fish Hatchery along Forest Service Road 69. This hatchery is a main source for thousands of trout for North Georgia streams and is open to the public.

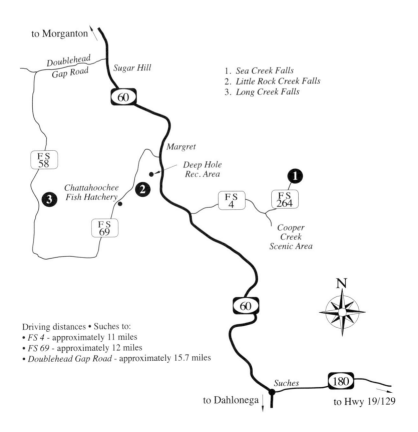

1. *Sea Creek Falls*
2. *Little Rock Creek Falls*
3. *Long Creek Falls*

Driving distances • Suches to:
• *FS 4* - approximately 11 miles
• *FS 69* - approximately 12 miles
• *Doublehead Gap Road* - approximately 15.7 miles

Sea Creek Falls

Stream: Sea Creek
Rating: good
Type: cascade
Height: 25 feet
Stream flow: medium

USGS Quad: Mulky Gap, GA
Landowner: Chattahoochee National Forest
Trail length: .25 mile (one way)
Difficulty: moderate
Elevation: 2,220 feet

Directions

From Suches take Hwy. 60 north for approximately 11 miles. Turn right onto Cooper Creek Road at the Cooper Creek Store. Proceed 3 miles to FS 264 on the left. Proceed 0.1 mile to the point where the road is blocked and park adjacent to the Sea Creek ford. Note: FS 264 can be quite rough and some of the mud holes could present problems for passenger vehicles in wet weather.

Trail and description

Sea Creek Falls is a surprisingly pretty cascade that's a bit off the beaten path but actually fairly easy to reach. An overgrown trail follows an old road from the parking area about 0.25 mile upstream along the left side of the creek. It ends at a shallow plunge pool at the base of the playful 25-foot drop. A steep primitive path with a few hazardous drop-offs ascends the left bank to a nice vantage point. Viewing the falls from "ground level" requires a bit of wading into the shallow plunge pool, which is actually somewhat of a reward in the warm summer months.

Sea Creek Falls

Little Rock Creek Falls

Stream: Little Rock Creek   USGS Quad: Noontootla, GA
Rating: excellent   Landowner: Chattahoochee National Forest
Type: cascade   Trail length: .4 mile (one way)
Height: 25 feet   Difficulty: moderate (not for children)
Stream flow: medium   Elevation: 2,570 feet

Directions

From Suches take Hwy. 60 north for approximately 12 miles and turn left onto Rock Creek Road (FS 69) just past the Deep Hole Recreation Area. Proceed 3.4 miles and park on the left side of the road at the Little Rock Creek bridge.

Trail and description

Just a few years ago the path leading up to the scenic cascade on Little Ridge Creek was difficult to locate, much less follow. Today the path is fairly well-worn and not too difficult, but it does require some scrambling over fallen trees. It also requires a bit of uphill climbing but nothing too tough.

Once you arrive at the waterfall you must scramble down a slippery path to the boulder-strewn base. This cascade is surprisingly powerful as it roars over a series of steep ledges into a narrow mist-laden cove littered with boulders. This is definitely not a good waterfall for small children, and even adults will get a bit dirty from all the scrambling required to get a good view.

This is also a good time to remind hikers of one of the most underrated dangers in the woods: bees and hornets. I was stung over 40 times by hornets while visiting this waterfall in 2009. The hornets had built a nest on a rhododendron limb alongside the scramble path just above the plunge pool and it was virtually invisible until I brushed against it. If you are allergic to bee stings be sure to take your medications with you into the woods.

Little Rock Creek Falls

Long Creek Falls

Stream: Long Creek
Rating: excellent
Type: cascade
Height: 20 feet
Stream flow: medium

USGS Quad: Noontootla, GA
Landowner: Chattahoochee National Forest
Trail length: 1 mile (one way)
Difficulty: moderate
Elevation: 2,830 feet

Directions

From Suches take Hwy. 60 north for approximately 15.7 miles. Turn
left onto Doublehead Gap Road and proceed 5.7 miles to FS 58. Turn left and
proceed approximately 5.5 miles to the Appalachian Trail at Three Forks. Park
here.

Trail and description

Long Creek Falls is a popular camping site for hikers enjoying the
Appalachian Trail, Duncan Ridge Trail and Benton MacKaye Trail. This
portion of the Appalachian Trail is only about 6 miles north of the southern
terminus at Springer Mountain so trail traffic is understandably heavy. The
Three Forks area is named for the junction of Long Creek, Chester Creek and
Stover Creek. The three streams combine to form Noontootla Creek. This area
is not to be confused with the other Three Forks in North Georgia in the West
Fork Chattooga River watershed in Rabun County.

To reach Long Creek Falls walk northeast over a series of low ridges.
At about the one mile point after a short, steep ascent, look for a marked side
trail to the left. This trail leads about 100 yards up to the pretty 20-foot cascade.
The side trail to Long Creek Falls also marks the starting point for the Duncan
Ridge Trail; it also happens to be the junction where the Benton MacKaye Trail
separates from the Appalachian Trail after sharing a common pathway.

*late summer brings low
water to Long Creek Falls*

Georgia Hub #4 - Helen to Unicoi Gap

      The alpine village of Helen makes a great starting point for a number of Georgia's most well-known waterfalls. The town is one of the most popular destinations in North Georgia and is home to dozens of events throughout the year. Just a few minutes north is beautiful Unicoi State Park, one of the most heavily visited state parks in Georgia. Just north of the park is Anna Ruby Falls, one of Georgia's most well-known waterfalls. The magnificent Richard Russell Scenic Highway begins just a few miles west of town, offering up several wonderful waterfalls and nearly twenty miles of incomparable mountain views.

      The main north/south artery through this portion of the mountains is busy Georgia Highway 17/75 which features nearly twenty miles of superb

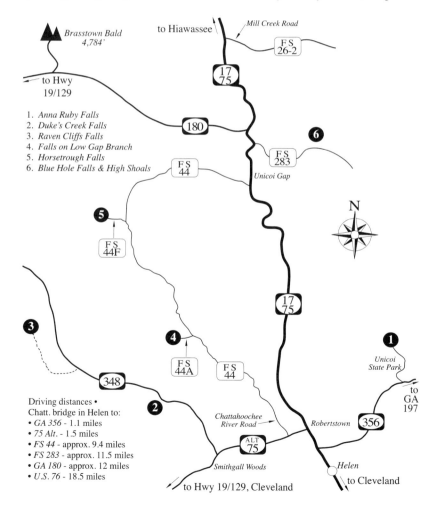

mountain scenery between Helen and Hiawassee. Approximately halfway between these two towns the famous Appalachian Trail crosses the highway at Unicoi Gap. Several miles north of Unicoi Gap Georgia Hwy. 180 heads west to a spur which takes visitors to the top of Georgia's highest peak, Brasstown Bald (4,784'). The final six miles winds through the scenic valley of the Hiawassee River before intersecting U.S. 76 on the outskirts of Hiawassee. Hiawassee is popular both with tourists and with those who have relocated in order to live on beautiful Lake Chatuge.

Anna Ruby Falls ★

Stream: York and Curtis Creeks
Rating: excellent
Type: cascade and free-falling
Height: 153 feet, 50 feet
Stream flow: medium

USGS Quad: Tray Mountain, GA
Landowner: Anna Ruby Falls Scenic Area
Trail length: 0.4 mile (one way)
Difficulty: moderate (paved)
Elevation: 2,000 feet

Directions

From the Chattahoochee River bridge in Helen proceed north on Hwy. 17/75 for 1.1 miles and turn right onto GA 356. Drive 1.4 miles, then turn left into Unicoi State Park on FS 242. Drive 3.5 miles to the parking lot. Visitors will pass an entrance kiosk for Unicoi State Park (you will not be required to pay here unless you plan to utilize the park's facilities) before reaching Anna Ruby Falls Scenic Area (administered by the U.S. Forest Service). Waterfall visitors will have to pay a nominal entrance fee to enter.

Trail and description

Anna Ruby Falls is one of the most beautiful waterfalls in Georgia, and also one of the most heavily visited. Not only is it close to a major tourist town (Helen) but its location adjacent to Unicoi State Park makes it a major destination for North Georgia tourists. Each year tens of thousands of visitors come to this beautiful 1,600-acre scenic area to enjoy the rare twin waterfalls and cascading stream found on the lower slopes of mighty Tray Mountain.

The waterfalls are named for Anna Ruby Nichols, the only daughter of Colonel John H. Nichols. Nichols settled in the Sautee-Nacoochee valley just south of Helen after the Civil War. Nichols built the beautiful Victorian home "West End" which is now owned by the state and recently renovated. The beautiful home is located at the intersection of Hwy. 17 and Hwy. 75 just south of Helen across from the historic Nacoochee Indian mound. Nichols once owned much of the land in the area and he and Anna Ruby spent countless hours exploring this magnificent wilderness. More on the colorful history of the people and land can be found during your visit here.

The larger of the two falls is the 153-foot combination water slide and steep cascade on Curtis Creek. Just a few yards away York Creek plunges over a 50-foot sheer drop into a boulder-filled ravine. These two pristine mountain streams converge just below their respective falls and give birth to frolicking Smith Creek.

A paved 0.4 mile interpretive path leads up to the falls. It consists of a gentle uphill walk with one steep stretch near the end. You might huff and puff just a bit but there are plenty of spots to stop along the way to enjoy the crashing mountain stream alongside the path. A footbridge and an upper and lower observation deck provides great views of the falls.

The Cradle of Forestry Interpretive Association operates a gift shop and visitor's center at the trailhead. U.S. Forest Service personnel are normally on hand to answer any questions you may have. Don't forget to bring your picnic basket. The creekside picnic area is one of the best in North Georgia.

Anna Ruby Falls

Dukes Creek Falls ★

Stream: Davis Creek   USGS Quad: Cowrock, GA
Rating: excellent   Landowner: Chattahoochee National Forest
Type: steep cascade   Trail length: 1.1 mile (one way)
Height: 200 feet   Difficulty: moderate
Stream flow: small   Elevation: 1,800 feet

Directions

From the Chattahoochee River bridge in Helen proceed north on Hwy. 17/75 for 1.5 miles and turn left onto 75 Alt. Proceed 2.3 miles and turn right onto GA Hwy 348 (Richard Russell Scenic Highway). Drive 1.7 miles to the Duke's Creek Falls parking area on the left. The Forest Service charges a nominal parking fee.

Trail and description

The name Dukes Creek Falls is a bit misleading. This 200-foot cascade actually occurs on Davis Creek. The waterfall is set in a magnificent gorge charged with the sights, sounds and smells of falling water. Actually the waters of Davis Creek merge with Dodd Creek to form Dukes Creek. That's a lot of "d's" but don't miss the point: this is a darned wonderful area to visit.

*early spring view of
Dukes Creek Falls*

observation deck
overlooking Dodd Creek

From the far end of the parking loop, locate the path for the 1.1 mile descent into the gorge. As the path skirts the edge of the parking area an elongated wooden walkway offers a long range view (approximately 300 yards) of the upper cascades of Dukes Creek Falls. The ever present sounds of rushing water far below provide just a hint of the experience ahead. At approximately .35 mile, the trail encounters a flight of steps. At the base, the trail turns sharply left and follows an old road bed while it parallels plunging Dodd Creek downstream for a half mile. At the .85 mile point the trail makes a hard right turn as it leaves the roadway and continues to descend along a narrow path toward the base of the waterfall.

Anyone who has not visited this waterfall in a decade or more will be surprised when they see the incredible observation platform that has been constructed at the base of the gorge. This structure features a wooden walkway several hundred feet long that connects two viewing platforms. One looks out across Dodd Creek toward the lower cascades of Dukes Creek Falls (somewhat obscured by heavy streamside foliage). At the far end of the walkway another deck offers a view upstream of a powerful 15-foot cascade on thundering Dodd Creek. This is a spot to linger and immerse the senses. I recently saw a father and two little boys throw a fishing line off the observation deck into the rushing creek and immediately pull a nice rainbow trout out of the creek.

Raven Cliffs Falls ★

Stream: Dodd Creek
Rating: excellent
Type: cascade/free fall
Height: 50 feet
Stream flow: small

USGS Quad: Cowrock, GA
Landowner: Mark Trail Wilderness
Trail length: 2.5 miles (one way)
Difficulty: moderate
Elevation: 2,590 feet

Directions

From the Chattahoochee River bridge in Helen proceed north on Hwy. 17/75 for 1.5 miles and turn left onto 75 Alt. Proceed 2.3 miles and turn right onto GA Hwy 348 (Richard Russell Scenic Highway). Drive 2.9 miles and turn left onto the parking access road. Proceed several hundred yards and park.

Trail and description

The beautiful 5 mile round trip hike to Raven Cliffs Falls is one of the most popular day hikes in North Georgia. The vast majority of the hike is alongside tumbling Dodd Creek. The trail passes several small waterfalls and scores of smaller shoals en route to Raven Cliffs. At the end of the trail is one of the southern Appalachians most unusual waterfalls - Raven Cliffs Falls.

From the large developed parking area just off the Russell Scenic Highway head into the woods following the creek upstream. The tone for this hike is set early as you pass a small waterfall just upstream of the wooden

Raven Cliffs Falls

*Dodd Creek
cascade at mile 1.4*

footbridge near the trailhead. The forest scenery is magnificent with plenty of lush rhododendron, laurel and native hemlock. Wildflowers are plentiful in the spring and summer months, enhancing the beautiful streamside environment.

   The first waterfall worthy of note occurs just over one mile from the trailhead. This pretty 12-foot drop spills into an open area scoured down to bedrock. A steep path descends to the base for an unobstructed view, but exercise extreme caution - the rocks are very slippery here. A larger cascade occurs at mile 1.4. This impressive 25-foot cascade should be enjoyed from the safety of the trail. Though a steep scramble path descends to the base, I really cannot recommend exploring this area.

   At mile 2.4 the path climbs into a narrow ravine. A series of noisy cascades emanates from a massive grey cliff which fills the upper end of the ravine. As the trail nears the cliff a huge vertical cleft opens in the rock face and Raven Cliffs Falls is revealed. A small opening in the rock focuses the stream into a narrow chute as it drops into the dark cleft. Because the light is poor inside the rock the waterfall can be a bit tough to photograph.

   Adventurous hikers not afraid of heights may want to tackle the climb to the top of the cliffs. A primitive path runs up the right side of the cliffs and a maze of exposed roots serve as hand holds as you make your way up and down. This is a potentially dangerous climb and is definitely not for small children. Atop the cliffs there are no rails, so use extreme caution. The top of the cliffs not only offers great views of the valley below, but there is yet another surprise just upstream as an additional cascade on Dodd Creek tumbles down into the back side of Raven Cliffs.

Other Falls in the Raven Cliffs Area

A small, scenic cascade can by reached by continuing on the gravel road for one mile past the Raven Cliffs Falls parking area to a shallow ford on Davis Creek (may not be suitable for passenger vehicles). Cross the creek, turn right and walk upstream for about 100 yards to the small falls.

Falls on Low Gap Branch

Stream: Low Gap Branch   USGS Quad: Jack's Gap, GA
Rating: good   Landowner: Chattahoochee WMA
Type: cascade   Trail length: 0.9 miles (one way)
Height: 15 feet   Difficulty: moderate (no real trail)
Stream flow: small   Elevation: 2,140 feet

Directions
From the Chattahoochee River bridge in Helen proceed north on Hwy. 17/75 for 1.5 miles and turn left onto 75 Alt. Immediately turn right onto Chattahoochee River Road, which starts as paved but turns into unpaved FS 44. Proceed 4.4 miles to FS 44A on the left. Turn here and proceed 0.7 mile and park just before the second ford.

Trail and description
If trails aren't your thing and scrambling through the woods is more to your liking, the small cascade on Low Gap Branch may be your ticket. From the primitive parking area preceding the second ford, walk across the stream on the low water concrete bridge and head upstream along a faint trail which begins behind the vehicle-blocking boulders. Pick your way upstream for approximately 0.3 mile, passing through dense rhododendron thickets and somewhat open woods.

*Low Gap Branch
cascade*

When the path reaches England Camp Branch which enters from the left, step across Low Gap Branch and begin working your way upstream along the east bank. Initially there is a reasonable path, but as the path peters out the easiest route is to angle uphill away from the thick streamside underbrush. Proceed about 0.3 mile, crossing two small branches within steep ravines along the way. Descend toward the roaring of the 15-foot cascade. This waterfall takes a bit of work, and the route is more difficult during the warm weather months; stream fordings may make a cold weather visit impractical.

Horsetrough Falls ★

Stream: Little Horsetrough Creek
Rating: Excellent
Type: cascade
Height: 75 feet
Stream flow: Small

USGS Quad: Jack's Gap, GA
Landowner: Mark Trail Wilderness
Trail length: 200 yards (one way)
Difficulty: Easy
Elevation: 2,300 feet

Directions

From the Chattahoochee River bridge in Helen proceed north on Hwy. 17/75 for 1.5 miles and turn left onto 75 Alt. Immediately turn right onto Chattahoochee River Road (which has been signed "Poplar Stump Road" at times), which starts as paved but turns into unpaved FS 44. Proceed 4.4 miles to the FS 44A junction, then continue approximately 5.7 miles to the Upper Chattahoochee River campground.

A more direct route (if you only intend to visit Horsetrough Falls) is to take Hwy 17/75 out of Helen for 9.4 miles. Turn left onto FS 44 just before Unicoi Gap and drive 4.75 miles to FS 44-F. Turn right here and drive to the far end of the campground loop to the Horsetrough Falls trailhead.

Description

In my opinion this is one of the area's most scenic cascades *if* you catch it at the right time. Water level makes all the difference here as Horsetrough Creek is quite small. During high flow periods the entire face of the cliff becomes alive with a cascading veil of falling water. The drive is a bit tedious, but the payoff comes in smaller crowds. Some changes over the last decade or so turned the Horsetrough "hike" into a 200 yard stroll. From the parking area at the upper end of the campground loop, look for the green sign designating trail #173. Follow the flat path for about 150 feet up to a small wooden footbridge which crosses the renowned Chattahoochee River, primary supplier of mighty Lake Lanier and the source of most of Atlanta's drinking water. The river is really only a small stream at this point, originating just a few miles upstream. Beyond the bridge continue along the path for an additional 150 yards to a large observation deck downstream of the waterfall. Resist the urge to approach the falls, as the rocks are treacherously slippery! The beauty of Horsetrough Falls is best enjoyed from afar.

Horsetrough Falls

Other Falls in the Horsetrough Falls Area

The Chattahoochee River pours through a narrow cleft in the riverbed into a secluded grotto just a few hundred yards north of the Horsetrough Falls trail. From the trailhead parking area in the upper Chattahoochee River campground loop, take trail #173 for about 50 yards up to the footbridge over the Chattahoochee. Just before you cross the bridge turn right and follow the path upstream for about 200 yards to the base of the falls. It's not a major drop by any means but the area is quite scenic and the small waterfall is surprisingly powerful.

Falls on High Shoals Creek ★

Stream: High Shoals Creek

Rating: excellent

Type: free-fall & cascade

Height: 15 feet, 100 feet

Stream flow: medium

USGS Quad: Tray Mountain, GA

Landowner: High Shoals Scenic Area

Trail length: 1 mile (one way)

Difficulty: Moderate (elevation change)

Elevation: 2,880 feet

Directions

From the Chattahoochee River bridge in Helen proceed north on Hwy. 17/75 for approximately 11.5 miles. Turn right onto FS 283 and proceed 1.4 bumpy miles to a small parking area on the left. Note: vehicles must ford the tiny Hiawassee River just a few hundred yards from the highway turn off. Under most conditions this should not present much of a problem.

Trail and description

The 170-acre High Shoals Scenic Area is home to two captivating waterfalls separated by only a few hundred yards of inaccessible stream. The hike to the falls is only about one mile, but the real kicker here is the several hundred foot change in elevation. It's nearly all downhill on the way to the falls, so coming back out is the only real challenge.

From the tiny parking area along FS 283 a green marker denotes Trail #19. The path immediately begins a descent into the steep north facing cove along a protracted series of gentle switchbacks. At 0.5 mile the path reaches splashing High Shoals Creek and crosses a wooden footbridge. The trail then levels out as it follows the creek downstream along an old road bed through a primitive camping area. At 0.9 mile the trail begins to descend again. At about

Blue Hole Falls

the one mile point look for a large rock on the right. Just ahead on the left is a short side trail that drops down to an observation platform directly across from beautiful **Blue Hole Falls**.

At Blue Hole Falls the High Shoals Creek takes a 15-foot sheer drop into a deep plunge pool. It is perfectly framed by lush streamside foliage and is a perfect spot to linger. Blue Hole's plunge pool is extremely deep and on more than one occasion I have witnessed misguided individuals diving from the brink of the falls into the pool. Quite a few deaths have occurred at these falls, more than enough reason to view them from the safety of the observation decks.

Wild and rugged High Shoals Falls

Leaving Blue Hole, backtrack to the main trail, turn left and continue downhill for 0.1 mile. At this point the trail turns sharply left and leaves the old roadbed. Descend along the rocky path for several hundred yards along a series of switchbacks to the observation deck at the base of **High Shoals Falls**.

To be so close and located on the same creek these two falls could not be more different. Whereas Blue Hole has a classic symmetrical form and deep plunge pool, High Shoals is a confusing chaos of falling water and fragmented rock. It begins as a narrow flume but quickly spreads out to cover much of the cliff face at high water. There are a few good "roostertails" that spray water vertically from the rock face. On the downside, this is yet another location where you will see idiotic behavior on display; stay off the rocks here and by all means do not climb the waterfall!

Georgia Hub #5 - The lower Tallulah basin

If you like to visit a wide variety of waterfalls in a relatively small area it's hard to beat the waterfalls in the Tallulah River basin in northeast Georgia. While the waterfalls of the upper Tallulah River above Lake Burton are not included in this hub, I've decided to include one waterfall that is not in the Tallulah basin - Toccoa Falls - simply because it is a major waterfall and is located about 15 minutes from Tallulah Falls.

Large, small, narrow, wide - you name it, you'll find it in this hub. From the free-falling majesty of Toccoa Falls to the intimate cascades of Angel Falls, this is a great collection of waterfalls. In addition, this region is one of the most popular tourist destinations for many other reasons. To start, rugged Tallulah Gorge tears a dramatic gash in the southern flank of the Blue Ridge that is nearly 2 miles long and 1,000-feet deep. Tallulah Gorge State Park is a popular destination not only for waterfall lovers, but features something for everyone - hikers, boaters, fishermen, campers, and the list goes on.

Above and below the gorge is a splendid string of Georgia's "great lakes": Burton, Seed, Rabun, Tallulah, Tugalo, and Yonah. These lakes provide the setting for hundreds of upscale vacation and retirement homes but also attract thousands of visitors each year who come to enjoy boating, fishing and swimming in these incomparable waters.

Peaceful Moccasin Creek State Park is nestled on the beautiful western shoreline of Lake Burton, but if you want to camp here you had better make your reservations months in advance. Besides camping and boating, trout fishing is popular on splashing Moccasin Creek which flows along the park's southern boundary. Moccasin Creek is also home to Hemlock Falls, one of this hub's featured falls.

The two towns closest to Tallulah Falls, Clarkesville to the south and Clayton to the north, are both popular destinations and feature vibrant, tourist-friendly downtowns. Both towns offer a full slate of seasonal festivals and events.

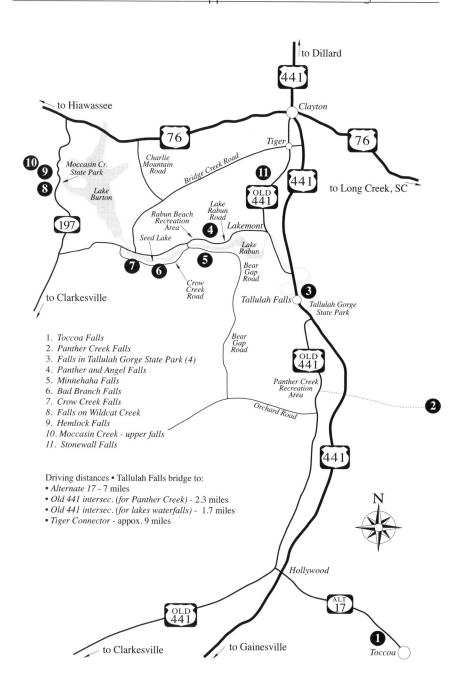

to Dillard

441

Clayton

to Hiawassee

76

Tiger

76

Charlie
Mountain
Road

Bridge Creek Road

to Long Creek, SC

441

Moccasin Cr.
State Park

OLD
441

Lake
Burton

Lake
Rabun
Road

197

Rabun Beach
Recreation
Area

Lakemont

Seed Lake

Lake
Rabun

Crow
Creek
Road

Bear
Gap
Road

to Clarkesville

Tallulah Falls

Tallulah Gorge
State Park

1. Toccoa Falls
2. Panther Creek Falls
3. Falls in Tallulah Gorge State Park (4)
4. Panther and Angel Falls
5. Minnehaha Falls
6. Bad Branch Falls
7. Crow Creek Falls
8. Falls on Wildcat Creek
9. Hemlock Falls
10. Moccasin Creek - upper falls
11. Stonewall Falls

Bear
Gap
Road

OLD
441

Panther Creek
Recreation
Area

Orchard Road

Driving distances • Tallulah Falls bridge to:
• Alternate 17 - 7 miles
• Old 441 intersec. (for Panther Creek) - 2.3 miles
• Old 441 intersec. (for lakes waterfalls) - 1.7 miles
• Tiger Connector - appox. 9 miles

441

N

Hollywood

OLD
441

ALT
17

to Clarkesville

to Gainesville

Toccoa

Toccoa Falls ★

Stream: Toccoa Creek	USGS Quad: Toccoa, GA
Rating: excellent	Landowner: Toccoa Falls College
Type: free-fall	Trail length: 200 yards (one way)
Height: 186 feet	Difficulty: easy
Stream flow: medium	Elevation: 880 feet

Directions

Toccoa Falls College is located about 1.5 miles north of Toccoa on Alternate Hwy 17. If you are starting in Tallulah Falls, the distance from the highway bridge to Alt 17 in Hollywood is approximately 7 miles. Turn left and proceed approximately 8 miles to the entrance of Toccoa Falls College on the right. Proceed through campus to a stop sign, then continue along the creek to the Gate Cottage on the right. There is a nominal charge to visit the falls.

Description

Not only is Toccoa Falls extremely rare due to its unusual height (186') but it is one of a handful of major North Georgia waterfalls that actually free-falls for its entire length. "Toccoa" is thought to emanate from the Cherokee word meaning *beautiful* and this waterfall is certainly that as it spills gracefully over a sheer stained brown ledge into an elongated plunge pool lined with massive fragments of fallen rock.

autumn leaves and boulders at the base of Toccoa Falls

The waterfall is located on the beautiful campus of Toccoa Falls College. The path from the school's newly rebuilt Gate Cottage to the waterfall is only a few hundred yards long and is nicely graded to accommodate wheelchairs. The waterfall is particularly photogenic during early April when dozens of azaleas along the path are in bloom. This is also an ideal waterfall for young children and senior citizens.

Historical note:

In November, 1977, several days of torrential rain overwhelmed an earthen dam above the waterfall that stored millions of gallons of lake water. The dam breached causing a flash flood through the lower portions of the campus. Thirty-nine members of the campus community were killed. In some cases entire families were lost in the tragedy. As you visit, take a moment to pause at the memorial that stands alongside the path.

Panther Creek Falls ★

Stream: Panther Creek	USGS Quad: Tallulah Falls, GA
Rating: excellent	Landowner: Chattahoochee National Forest
Type: wide series of cascades	Trail length: 3.5 miles (one way)
Height: 75 feet total drop	Difficulty: moderate (elevation change)
Stream flow: medium	Elevation: approx. 1,000 feet

Directions

From the U.S. 441 bridge in Tallulah Falls proceed south for 2.3 miles. Turn right onto Old 441. Drive 1.5 miles and turn right into the Panther Creek Recreation Area parking lot. There may be a fee charged to park here.

Trail and description

Once overlooked among North Georgia's waterfalls, the hike to Panther Creek Falls is now one of Georgia's most popular wilderness walks. On any given warm-season weekend scores of cars fill the parking area and those that can't fit in are lined up along the Old 441 shoulder. Unfortunately, such heavy visitation has taken a toll on the area around the falls - please tread lightly.

The 3.5 mile hike, while lengthy by this book's standards, is really not too difficult. The hike involves a fair degree of elevation change, but for most of its length it is surprisingly gentle. Recent trail renovations include relocating one section to make it gentler. The pathway stays delightfully close to the splashing stream for most of its length and provides a wide variety of sights and sounds to fill the senses. Wildflowers abound and the display of mountain laurel blooming in May is tremendous.

A few particulars will keep you on the right track. The initial 1.5 miles of this trail is along the steep hillside on the north side of the creek. At mile 1.5 the trail crosses a wooden footbridge and traverses the creek bottom along the south side of the creek. At mile 2.3 you will pass a long section of splashing shoals that drop about 20 feet. Do not mistake these for the real deal, as Panther Creek Falls is *much* larger, and still a bit over a mile ahead. At mile 2.8 the trail climbs briefly and passes underneath a series of rock overhangs high above the creek. In several instances steel cables have been set as guardrails to keep hikers safely on the trail. Beyond mile 2.8 the trail flattens for about half a mile and passes the top of massive Panther Creek Falls at mile 3.5. Continue on the path for 100 yards as you descend steeply to a wooded floodplain facing the lower cascades and massive plunge pool.

Panther Creek Falls

The total run of Panther Creek Falls is approximately 350 feet with a total drop estimated at 75 feet. The final cascade, the portion visitors view as they look across the pool, is about 30 feet high and 50-60 feet across. At higher water levels in the early spring spray fills the air as thousands of gallons of water plunge down the cliff. This is a popular camping spot and you may feel like you are right in the middle of someone's campsite if you visit on a summer weekend. Additionally, portions of the trail are in poor shape, especially along the descent to the base of the falls. Use caution if you decide to venture out onto the rocks to view the upper cascades. One last hint: allow plenty of time for the return (uphill) climb out. It's definitely the harder half of the hike.

The Falls of Tallulah Gorge

If there were a such thing as waterfall nirvana in North Georgia it would probably be found at Tallulah Gorge State Park. Within the confines of this 2,739-acre park are five major waterfalls and several other smaller falls. Four of these falls are on the Tallulah River - Ladore, Tempesta, Hurricane and Oceana - and are visible from overlooks along the park's popular rim trails. Another, Bridal Veil (aka "Sliding Rock") is one of the only waterfalls you'll ever be encouraged to actually "ride."

One of the most interesting factoids about Tallulah Falls is that its waterfalls virtually disappeared for over eighty years. With the completion of Tallulah dam in 1913 the flow of the mighty Tallulah was silenced. The river was channeled into twin diversion tunnels which ran underground for nearly a mile down to the Tallulah hydroelectric plant at the far end of the gorge. Only a trickle of water seeped through the gorge, silencing the "Niagara of the South" as it was once known during its Victorian heyday in the 1880s and 1890s.

Tallulah Gorge State Park was founded in 1993 as a joint venture between the Georgia Department of Natural Resources and the Georgia Power Company. Not long afterwards a culvert was placed through the top of Tallulah dam allowing a constant 35 cfs (cubic feet per second) flow through the gorge. The banished waterfalls of Tallulah reappeared, though not at their former intensity. With the advent of whitewater releases (in early April and early November) releases of 500 - 700 cfs recreated the mighty Tallulah at full strength. Aesthetic releases are also scheduled throughout the year (check the park calendar) to allow more visitors to see the falls roar.

Tallulah Gorge #1 - L'Eau d'Or Falls ★

Stream: Tallulah River
Rating: excellent
Type: cascades
Height: 45 feet total drop
Stream flow: medium

USGS Quad: Tallulah Falls, GA
Landowner: Tallulah Gorge State Park
Trail length: 200 yards (one way)
Difficulty: easy
Elevation: 1,530 feet

Directions

From the U.S. 441 bridge in Tallulah Falls proceed north just around the next curve to the traffic light. Turn right onto Jane Hurt Yarn Road and proceed past the campground to the Jane Hurt Yarn Interpretive Center (park pass is required). Walk along the North Rim Trail behind the interpretive center for 200 yards to overlooks 2 and 3. Both provide a nice view of the falls from the safety of the rim from several hundred feet away.

L'Eau d'or Description

Of the five major waterfalls in Tallulah Gorge, L'Eau d'or (pronounced ladore) is one of the easiest to view. The name is French meaning *water of gold* and a visit here late in the afternoon may provide the source of the inspiration as sunlight gives a spectacular backlighting to the waterfall. A "rubberized" walkway manufactured from scrapped tires begins behind the Jane Hurt Yarn Interpretive Center and extends several hundred yards out to overlooks 2 and 3. Both overlooks provide a nice view of the beautiful 45-foot tall cascade from several hundred feet above. The emerald-green pool below the cascade is known as Hawthorne's Pool and is named for a minister who mysteriously vanished here after swimming alone. If the scene looks eerily familiar, perhaps it is because several key scenes from the 1972 film *Deliverance* were filmed here featuring the waterfall, pool, and cliffs.

L'Eau d'or Falls as seen from the North Rim Trail.

Tallulah Gorge #2 - Tempesta Falls ★

Stream: Tallulah River
Rating: excellent
Type: steep cascade
Height: 76 feet total drop
Stream flow: medium

USGS Quad: Tallulah Falls, GA
Landowner: Tallulah Gorge State Park
Trail length: 0.8 mile (one way)
Difficulty: easy to moderate
Elevation: 1,460 feet

Directions

Follow the directions previously given to the Jane Hurt Yarn Interpretive Center. Locate the North Rim Trail behind the center and head to the right. Continue past the L'Eau d'or overlooks for about 0.5 mile to the highway bridge. Climb the stairs to the right just before you pass under the bridge. Turn left and follow the South Rim Trail across the highway bridge, then veer left from the highway along the sidewalk. The first overlook to the left (#6 - under the old picnic pavilion) looks down onto Hawthorne's Pool and the top of Tempesta. Continue several hundred yards to overlook #7.

Description
    The Tallulah River pauses momentarily below L'Eau d'or before continuing its dizzying descent over 76-foot Tempesta Falls. This is an appropriate name for the waterfall as it funnels into a rocketing flume of falling water before crashing into the rocks at the base of the drop. Overlook #7 perfectly frames this impressive cascade.

*Tempesta Falls from
the South Rim Trail.*

Tallulah Gorge #3 - Hurricane Falls ★

Stream: Tallulah River
Rating: excellent
Type: steep cascade
Height: 96 feet total drop
Stream flow: medium

USGS Quad: Tallulah Falls, GA
Landowner: Tallulah Gorge State Park
Trail length: 1 mile to rim overlook (one way)
Difficulty: moderate
Elevation: 1,360 feet

Directions
    Follow the directions previously given to the Jane Hurt Yarn Interpretive Center. Locate the North Rim Trail behind the center and head to the right. Continue to the highway bridge, then take the South Rim Trail approximately one-half mile to overlook #8.

Trail and description

Many visitors find that 96-foot Hurricane Falls is the most impressive of the Tallulah's major cascades. While it is a beautiful waterfall at normal river levels during a whitewater release it is transformed into a mass of churning thunder as the river consumes nearly every square foot of the cliff face. If you are ever in the area when there has been excessive rain and Georgia Power is releasing water over the dam, you need to view Hurricane Falls as it borders on the insane. The mist from the waterfall becomes so heavy that it obscures the cliff face opposite the plunge pool.

For those looking for a great workout, Hurricane's base is accessible via the park's stairway system into the gorge. The stairs actually provide a "shortcut" between the north and south rim trails. From overlook #2 on the north rim, take the stairway down (approximately 310 stairs) to a spectacular suspension bridge perched nearly 100 feet above the gorge floor just above the brink of Hurricane Falls. The climb back out to the south rim from the bridge is a heart-pounding 347 steps.

If you're thirsty for more, you can descend from the bridge to the base of Hurricane Falls. From the south end of the bridge take the stairway down another 225 steps to the bottom. A large observation platform perched above the massive plunge pool provides an excellent vantage point. Hikers with gorge floor permits get an even better view of Hurricane Falls as they scramble across the river to make the half-mile journey downstream to Sliding Rock.

*Hurricane Falls as seen from the river crossing
en route to Oceana Falls and Sliding Rock.*

Tallulah Gorge #4 - Oceana Falls

Stream: Tallulah River
Rating: excellent
Type: steep waterslide
Height: 50 feet total drop
Stream flow: medium

USGS Quad: Tallulah Falls, GA
Landowner: Tallulah Gorge State Park
Trail length: 0.25 mile to rim overlook (one way)
Difficulty: easy
Elevation: 1,300 feet

Directions

Follow the directions previously given to the Jane Hurt Yarn Interpretive Center. Locate the North Rim Trail behind the center and turn left. Walk about one quarter mile to overlook #1. This portion of the trail requires visitors to walk down several dozen stairs.

Oceana Falls, during a whitewater release from overlook #1

Trail and description

Overlook #1 provides stunning views into the gorge's "grand avenue" section, the heart of the gorge. This overlook is approximately 750 feet above the river and looks directly down onto Oceana Falls. Oceana is formed by a huge 50-foot river-wide ledge tilted at approximately forty-five degrees. This waterfall lives up to its name at high water levels when the entire ledge surges and boils with a wall of falling water.

From the vantage point of overlook #1 you cannot obtain an accurate perspective of how tall this cascade is. In my opinion, of the five major waterfalls Oceana is possibly the most misleading at normal water levels. Rim hikers now have another option for viewing Oceana. The park recently (summer 2010) opened a spur trail leading to Point Inspiration, the highest overlook on the gorge rim. This point is a bit further downstream and gives a better angle to view the cascade. To reach Point Inspiration look for the signs leading into the woods at the far end of overlook #1. Walk 0.25 mile ascending approximately 200 feet to the overlook perched high atop the north rim cliffs.

Tallulah Gorge #5 - Bridal Veil Falls

Stream: Tallulah River
Rating: excellent
Type: steep waterslide
Height: 15 feet total drop
Stream flow: medium

USGS Quad: Tallulah Falls, GA
Landowner: Tallulah Gorge State Park
Trail length: 1 mile (one way)
Difficulty: difficult/strenuous
Elevation: 1,275 feet

Directions

Follow the directions previously given to the Jane Hurt Yarn Interpretive Center. Obtain a gorge floor permit (mandatory). Locate the North Rim Trail behind the center and turn right. Walk to overlook #2 then descend approximately 535 stairs to the base of Hurricane Falls. Exit the stairs and pick your way across the river. Work downstream along the left bank of the river for 0.5 mile to Bridal Veil Falls.

Note: This is a difficult and potentially dangerous hike. There have been scores of injuries and numerous fatalities in the gorge. You must be in good physical condition and properly equipped (proper shoes/plenty of drinking water) to make this hike. Consult park personnel at the information desk in the Yarn Interpretive Center for more details.

Trail and description

Bridal Veil Falls, as the name implies, gracefully fans out across a rounded 15-foot ledge and spills into a massive boulder-lined plunge pool beneath towering grey cliffs. This is a spectacularly beautiful area. Bridal Veil is affectionately known as "Sliding Rock" and is the only location in the gorge where swimming is allowed. In fact, swimming and sliding could be considered mandatory activities here. One hundred visitors per day are allowed onto the gorge floor, and nearly all of them end up taking the plunge at Sliding Rock. Be careful, the water-polished rocks *are very slippery!*

*Bridal Veil Falls,
aka "Sliding Rock"*

Panther and Angel Falls

Stream: Joe Branch   USGS Quad: Tiger, GA
Rating: excellent   Landowner: Rabun Beach Campground
Type: cascades   Trail length: 1 mile (one way) to Angel Falls
Height: 50 feet   Difficulty: moderate
Stream flow: small   Elevation: 2,100, 2,300 feet

Directions

From the highway bridge in Tallulah Falls drive north on U.S. 441 for
1.7 miles. Turn onto Old 441 at the Lake Rabun Recreation Area sign. Proceed
2.4 miles and turn left onto Lake Rabun Road. Proceed 4.5 miles to Rabun
Beach Camping Area #2. Drive slowly around the campground loop to the day
use parking area at the upper end of the loop. There is a day use fee required.

*Panther Falls
on the Joe
Branch Trail*

Trail and description

The scenic Joe Branch Trail features two pretty cascades along a
moderately strenuous one mile (one way) trail leading north from the Rabun
Beach campground. The trail closely follows tumbling Joe Branch for is entire
length. The trail climbs for most of its length and you'll definitely get a good
workout as you ascend into the narrow Joe Branch watershed.

The first waterfall is Panther Falls; it occurs 0.6 mile from the trailhead. Panther is the larger of the two falls, tumbling in picture-perfect fashion over a ledge of highly striated rock. A bench has been placed a few yards from the base by a tiny plunge pool. Take a minute to catch your breath because once you leave Panther Falls behind the trail climbs steeply for several hundred yards past the uppermost cascades of Panther Falls. It levels off somewhat for a few hundred yards giving you a bit of a breather before branching into a loop for the final approach to Angel Falls.

Angel Falls is a beautifully intricate cascade which tumbles gracefully over a series of tiny ledges in the bedrock. A footbridge rests just yards from the final cascades. It is perfectly framed within a lush envelope of streamside greenery.

Regarding water levels

Both of these waterfalls are quite beautiful when the creek level is moderate to high, but somewhat disappointing at low water. You may want to postpone your visit during prolonged dry spells.

trail's end at
beautiful Angel Falls

Minnehaha Falls ★

Stream: Fall Creek
Rating: excellent
Type: cascade
Height: 60 feet
Stream flow: medium

USGS Quad: Tallulah Falls, GA
Landowner: Chattahoochee National Forest
Trail length: 0.3 mile (one way)
Difficulty: easy
Elevation: 1,850 feet

Directions

Follow the directions to Panther and Angel Falls. Continue past Rabun Beach Campground #2 for an additional 1.7 miles (6.2 miles from Old 441). Turn left and cross the bridge just downstream of the Seed Lake dam. Proceed 150 yards and bear left onto Bear Gap Road. Proceed 1.6 miles along the southern shoreline of Lake Rabun to a small pull-off on the left. The trail begins across the road. There is normally a trailhead sign on the right.

Minnehaha Falls

Trail and description

Minnehaha definitely makes my top ten list of Georgia waterfalls. This cascade energetically tumbles down a steep series of intricate ledges into a picturesque cove. The trail is delightfully short and other than a few brief uphills it is not difficult. The base of the falls is broad and open, and several large rock slabs provide excellent spots to sit and enjoy the falls. Try to plan a visit during rhododendron season (mid-summer) and you'll be in for a treat. *Note:* avoid summer weekends like the plague(!) and try to resist the urge to climb on the waterfall; it's tempting but just too dangerous.

Bad Branch Falls

Stream: Bad Branch   USGS Quad: Lake Burton, GA
Rating: excellent   Landowner: Chattahoochee National Forest
Type: cascade   Trail length: 0.2 mile (one way)
Height: 20 feet   Difficulty: easy to moderate
Stream flow: small   Elevation: 1,950 feet

Directions

Follow the directions on the previous page to the bridge over the
Tallulah River just below the Seed Lake dam. Continue across the bridge and
proceed 0.25 mile. Turn right onto Crow Creek Road. Drive 2.9 miles to a
small pull-off. The unmarked trail begins on the left side of the road (the last
time I visited there was a marker here reading "Georgia Power Witness Post".

Trail and description

Several small scenic waterfalls are located along Crow Creek Road
near the southern shoreline of Seed Lake. The first, Bad Branch Falls, is a
small 20-foot cascade that tumbles over a fractured, slanting ledge onto a small
boulder pile. It's not a major waterfall, but well worth the 5 minute walk if
you're in the area. From the pull-off along Crow Creek Road follow the old
roadbed for several hundred yards up to the cascade.

Bad Branch Falls

Crow Creek Falls

Stream: Crow Creek
Rating: good
Type: cascade
Height: 10 feet
Stream flow: small

USGS Quad: Lake Burton, GA
Landowner: Chattahoochee National Forest
Trail length: 300 yards (one way)
Difficulty: moderate
Elevation: 1,840 feet

Directions

Follow the directions to Bad Branch Falls on the preceding page. Continue beyond the Bad Branch Falls pull-off for 2 additional miles (a total of 4.9 miles from the turn-off onto Crow Creek Road) to the point where Crow Creek flows under the road (be aware that there is another creek several hundred yards preceding Crow Creek). There is a path on the right side of the creek beyond several vehicle-blocking mounds. An additional landmark is a Forest Service road on the left just beyond the stream crossing.

Falls on Crow Creek

Trail and description

This is one of my favorite small falls in this book. The setting is green and lush. The cascade tumbles over a series of ledges onto a flat rock slab then continues over a series of smaller drops. At higher water levels another tongue of water develops to the right of the main drop. The rocks are moss covered and the sounds and smells are enchanting. Crow Creek Falls is a great place for a streamside picnic but avoid it if there are several other cars parked along the roadside - it simply can not handle crowds.

Falls on Wildcat Creek

Stream: Wildcat Creek
Rating: good
Type: cascade
Height: 15 feet
Stream flow: medium

USGS Quad: Tray Mountain, GA
Landowner: Chattahoochee National Forest
Trail length: upper - roadside
Difficulty: easy
Elevation: 2,110 feet

Directions

From Clayton take U.S. Hwy. 76 west for 11 miles. Turn left onto GA Hwy. 197 and drive 5 miles to West Wildcat Road (FS 127) on the right (1.4 miles south of Moccasin Creek State Park). Drive 1.4 miles to the falls on the left side of the road.

Sliding Rock on Wildcat Creek

Description

Two cascades on Wildcat Creek are located along West Wildcat Road. The first is affectionately known as "Sliding Rock." It's not as big as the one in Tallulah Gorge and not as crowded as the one in North Carolina, but it's easy and fun. This scenic 15-foot drop attracts large numbers of thrill seekers who slide down the falls into a broad, icy plunge pool. This spot draws big crowds of trout fishermen as well. About 100 yards downstream a long series of rushing cascades culminates in an obscure 20-foot waterfall. A steep, primitive path descends from the road to the general vicinity of the base.

Yet another smaller waterfall is located approximately 2.3 miles further up Wildcat Creek Road (3.8 miles total from Hwy. 197 and 0.4 mile above the third bridge). This cascade is only about 8-10 feet high but is quite pretty.

Hemlock Falls ★

Stream: Moccasin Creek
Rating: excellent
Type: cascade
Height: 12 feet
Stream flow: medium

USGS Quad: Lake Burton, GA
Landowner: Chattahoochee National Forest
Trail length: 1.0 mile (one way)
Difficulty: moderate
Elevation: 2,110 feet

Directions

From Clayton take U.S. 76 west for 11 miles. Turn left onto GA 197 and drive 3.7 miles to Moccasin Creek State Park. Just past the Moccasin Creek bridge turn right onto FS 165A at the Hemlock Falls sign and proceed 0.5 mile to a large dirt parking area at the end of the road.

Trail and description

The path to Hemlock Falls is a hiker's delight as it closely follows Moccasin Creek for about one mile up to the popular cascade. Trail #50 begins on the upper end of the large dirt parking area and follows the bed of an old logging railroad back into the watershed. The trail is always within earshot of the tumbling creek but draws progressively closer the further you walk. Several small brooks cross the path as it tunnels through the lush streamside foliage. A highlight of the hike occurs at 0.7 mile as the stream crosses a narrow wooden footbridge above rushing shoals. There are no railings on this bridge so be careful, especially if it is wet. Over the last few years one or two of the planks have disappeared as well. Years ago hikers had to ford the powerful stream which carried considerable risk.

Once along the right bank it is a moderately easy 0.3 mile walk up to the waterfall's massive plunge pool where the 30-foot wide waterfall tumbles in from the far right side. As the name implies the pool is lined with magnificent hemlocks as well as rhododendrons. A flat area cleared of underbrush is directly across from the cascade and provides a nice vantage point.

Hemlock Falls

Upper Falls on Moccasin Creek

Stream: Moccasin Creek
Rating: excellent
Type: cascade
Height: 25 feet
Stream flow: medium

USGS Quad: Tray Mountain, GA
Landowner: Chattahoochee National Forest
Trail length: 1.7 miles (one way)
Difficulty: difficult
Elevation: 2,450 feet

Directions

Follow the directions on the previous page to the Hemlock Falls trailhead.

Trail and description

If you're standing at Hemlock Falls and haven't even broken a sweat, you may be interested in the upper falls on Moccasin Creek located about 0.7 mile upstream. Be aware however, the *real* trail ends at Hemlock Falls. The rest of the way could be considered a path, but it's rough going.

If you're game continue past Hemlock Falls along the main trail to the streamside area above the waterfall. Rock hop across the stream and follow the faint path upstream, climbing up to the old rail bed once again. Along the way you'll have to cross several deep ravines where streams cross the path, but generally the "trail" stays well above rushing Moccasin Creek. The path also

upper falls on Moccasin Creek

passes through several interesting boulder fields en route to the falls. At mile 1.7 the cascade comes within earshot. Locate the steep side trail that drops down to stream level. Some scrambling over rocks is required to view the falls. Be very careful here as the area is isolated and the rocks are quite slick.

If you made it this far you'll be rewarded with a sublime wilderness scene as Moccasin Creek tumbles over a 25-foot ledge into a secluded plunge pool. The cascade is quite wide, perhaps 40 feet, and the pool is hemmed in downstream by large boulders.

Stonewall Falls

Stream: Stonewall Creek   USGS Quad: Tiger, GA
Rating: good   Landowner: Chattahoochee National Forest
Type: cascade   Trail length: 0.4 mile (one way)
Height: 10 feet   Difficulty: easy
Stream flow: medium   Elevation: 1,880 feet

Directions

From the Tallulah Falls bridge proceed north on U.S. 441 for 1.7 miles. Turn left onto Old 441 and proceed 5.7 miles to FS 20 on the left. Follow FS 20 for 1.3 miles to a parking area on the right for the Stonewall Falls biking trails. Continue on foot down FS 20 for 0.4 mile to the falls. Autos with good clearance can actually drive down to a turnaround just before the waterfall, but the road is quite rough and usually very muddy.

Stonewall Falls

Description

This pretty waterfall is located in an area where visitors camp just off the roadway. In the busy summer months you may pass a half dozen tents or more as you make your way down FS 20 to the waterfall. The waterfall is also located alongside the Stonewall Falls biking trail so you may see a few bicyclists fly by as well. It's a pretty cascade but the area gets crowded and is often quite trashy. As long as you're not expecting pristine wilderness perhaps you can still enjoy the beauty of the waterfall.

Georgia Hub #6 - Northwest Rabun County

Rabun County lies in the northeastern corner of Georgia and is home to some of the most beautiful mountain scenery in the Blue Ridge. In fact, *Outside* magazine once listed Rabun County as one of the 100 most beautiful counties in the country. Rabun boasts some of the South's most notable trails - the Appalachian, Bartram and the Chattooga River Trail. As previously noted the great lakes of Rabun are located here - Burton, Seed, Rabun, Tallulah and Tugalo. The county is home to the renowned Foxfire program as well as Georgia's highest state park - Black Rock Mountain State Park. The towns of Clayton and Dillard are popular tourist stops and there are dozens of great places to lodge and dine, including the world famous Dillard House.

The northwest corner of Rabun County features a number of excellent cascades (three listed in this hub are actually in North Carolina, but as they say, "you can't get there from here").

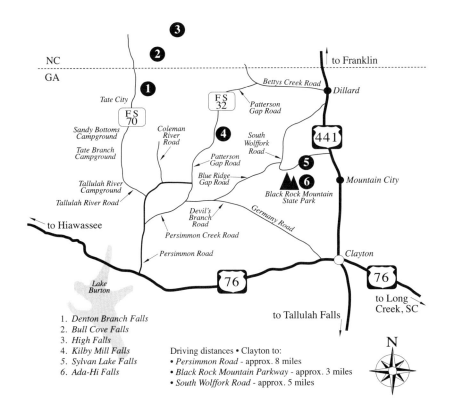

1. *Denton Branch Falls*
2. *Bull Cove Falls*
3. *High Falls*
4. *Kilby Mill Falls*
5. *Sylvan Lake Falls*
6. *Ada-Hi Falls*

Driving distances • Clayton to:
• *Persimmon Road* - approx. 8 miles
• *Black Rock Mountain Parkway* - approx. 3 miles
• *South Wolffork Road* - approx. 5 miles

Denton Branch Falls

Stream: Denton Branch
Rating: excellent
Type: steep cascade
Height: 25 feet
Stream flow: small

USGS Quad: Hightower Bald, NC, GA
Landowner: Southern Nantahala Wilderness
Trail length: 0.3 (one way)
Difficulty: easy
Elevation: 2,760 feet

Directions

From Clayton take U.S. 76 west for 8 miles. Turn right onto Persimmon Road and proceed 4.1 miles to Tallulah River Road (FS 70) on the left. Follow FS 70 for 6.5 miles to Denton Branch Road on the right (it may be unmarked). Drive up the narrow, bumpy road about 0.2 mile to a primitive camping area and park here.

Trail and description

Denton Branch Falls is a surprisingly powerful cascade which pours over a steep cliff into a shallow plunge basin. Begin by rock-hopping across Denton Branch just above the parking area. Follow the old roadbed for several hundred yards until the road bends left. Fork right here and follow a primitive path as it angles back toward the creek. Proceed 200 yards to the falls.

A tiny island located just downstream from the cascade provides a nice vantage point. If the creek is high a fair amount of spray and wind is generated around the base. Of special note is the sheer wall of rock to the left of the cascade that normally stays covered with seepage and dripping water.

*late summer
brings low water to
Denton Branch Falls*

Bull Cove Falls

Stream: Bull Cove Creek
Rating: good
Type: cascade
Height: 40 feet
Stream flow: small

USGS Quad: Rainbow Springs, NC, GA
Landowner: Southern Nantahala Wilderness
Trail length: 1 mile (one way)
Difficulty: moderate to strenuous
Elevation: 3,000 feet

Directions

From Clayton take U.S. 76 west for 8 miles. Turn right onto Persimmon Road and proceed 4.1 miles to Tallulah River Road (FS 70) on the left. Follow FS 70 7.8 miles (approximately 0.4 mile north of the GA/NC state line). Note: FS 70 becomes FS 56 at the NC line. Look for the Beech Creek Trail marker on the right. Park in the small clearing several hundred feet up the road on the left.

Trail and description

The rugged Beech Creek Loop Trail is a favorite among hikers as it offers challenging trails and wonderful wilderness scenery. Hikers who start from the southern trailhead are also treated to at least two worthy waterfalls within the first 2.5 miles. The first of the Beech Creek drainage cascades is Bull Cove Falls, located about one mile from the trailhead.

Beginning at the parking area along FS 56 walk south and look for the Beech Creek Trail sign on the eastern side of the road. The path immediately begins a steep 0.3 mile ascent up and over Scaly Ridge. The path then tackles a welcome 0.2 mile descent to splashing Beech Creek (which is normally not too difficult to rock-hop across). Cross the creek and continue up to the point where the trail intercepts an old logging road. Turn left and continue along the road for another half mile. At approximately one mile the trail crosses sparkling Bull Cove Creek. Step across to the north side of the creek and locate the primitive path that works its way upstream for about 100 yards to the cascade.

Bull Cove Falls powers its way over a slanting ledge, spilling into a cove cluttered with boulders and fallen logs. It's probably not worthy of a hike on its own merits but the waterfall makes a nice side trip for Beech Creek Loop hikers or as a primer for those hiking up to High Falls.

High Falls

Stream: Beech Creek
Rating: excellent
Type: cascade
Height: 150 feet
Stream flow: small

USGS Quad: Rainbow Springs, NC, GA
Landowner: Southern Nantahala Wilderness
Trail length: 2.4 miles (one way)
Difficulty: strenuous
Elevation: 3,000 feet

Directions

Follow the directions on the previous page to the Beech Creek Trail.

Trail and description

Isolated and beautiful, High Falls is a real gem and every serious waterfall bagger needs to visit this beauty at least once. High Falls doesn't share its secrets easily, as a strenuous 2.4 mile hike is required.

Refer to the trail description for Bull Cove Falls on the opposite page. Cross Bull Cove Creek and continue along the Beech Creek Trail. Rock hop or wade across Beech Creek at mile 1.2 and begin a relentless uphill walk for the balance of the journey to High Falls. Approximately 0.5 mile above the second Beech Creek crossing, Bear Creek Falls will appear high to your left as it cascades down a steep rock face before trickling across the trail and spilling into Beech Creek. This falls is a series of steep waterslides and much of it is hidden in the dense forest foliage. It's much easier to see in the leafless months of late fall and winter.

winter flow
at High Falls

Though the hike is arduous, Beech Creek Gorge rewards visitors with a magnificent setting full of natural beauty and a few historic attractions as well. At mile 2.3 the trail passes the remains of an old corundum mine on the left. Part of the original stacked stonework is still visible if you look closely.

At mile 2.4 the trail turns sharply left for a second time; look for the side path on the right. Normally there is a sign announcing the trail to the waterfall, but don't count on it. Follow this rough primitive path for about 250 yards down to the base of High Falls.

High Falls is a wonderfully rugged cascade and may exceed your expectations as it rushes down a stark, black cliff into a narrow cove. The cascade extends skyward well beyond the point you can actually see from the base. The total height is estimated at around 150 feet but only about half of it is visible from the base. The cascade fans out to perhaps 40 feet wide at the bottom. Periods of high water flow transform High Falls from simply a nice cascade to one that absolutely should not be missed.

Kilby Mill Falls

Stream: Kilby Mill Creek
Rating: good
Type: cascade
Height: 40 feet
Stream flow: small

USGS Quad: Dillard, GA, NC
Landowner: Coleman River WMA
Trail length: 0.3 miles (one way)
Difficulty: easy, but no maintained trail
Elevation: 2,140 feet

Directions

From Clayton take U.S. Hwy. 76 for 8 miles. Turn right onto Persimmon Road and drive 5 miles to the junction of Persimmon Road and Patterson Gap Road. Veer to the left and proceed 2.3 miles. Park in the pull-off just before you cross the bridge over Kilby Creek.

Trail and description

This scenic two-tiered cascade is a short walk from the roadside pull-off. Walk beyond the vehicle-blocking mounds of dirt and follow the old logging road east for 0.2 mile. Kilby Mill Creek soon veers off to the north; continue straight following a smaller branch upstream. Proceed several hundred feet and locate a path that crosses the branch. Walk a short distance through open woods to toward the sound of this scenic 40-foot cascade. The bottom tier is visible from the base, but the more impressive upper cascades can be viewed by following a steep path to the right.

Sylvan Falls

Stream: Taylor Creek   USGS Quad: Dillard, GA, NC
Rating: good   Landowner: Sylvan Falls Mill Bed & Breakfast
Type: cascade   Trail length: roadside
Height: 50 feet   Difficulty: n/a
Stream flow: small   Elevation: 2,180 feet

Directions

From Clayton take U.S. Hwy. 441 north for four miles. Turn left onto Wolffork Road and proceed 2.3 miles to Taylor's Chapel Road on the left. Proceed slowly up the narrow road and the Sylvan Falls Mill Bed & Breakfast will be on the right. The cascade is clearly visible to the left of the inn. Please respect that this is private property and do not trespass.

Description

Sylvan Falls is a pretty waterslide that tumbles down alongside historic old Sylvan Falls Mill. This restored structure once served as a private residence and now functions as a bed & breakfast. Of particular note is the enormous overshot waterwheel that has ground meal for over 150 years. The current owner of the bed & breakfast has done a very nice job reestablishing the grounds of the old mill. Beautiful plants and ornamental flowers in front of the inn accent the scene as the pretty 50-foot slide tumbles to the valley floor adjacent to the old mill. Be sure to ask permission if you would like to explore the grounds and view the cascade up close.

Sylvan Falls and the overshot waterwheel

Ada-hi Falls

Stream: Taylor Creek   USGS Quad: Dillard, GA, NC
Rating: good   Landowner: Black Rock Mountain State Park
Type: cascade   Trail length: 0.2 mile (one way)
Height: 50 feet   Difficulty: moderate (steps)
Stream flow: small   Elevation: 3,060 feet

Directions

From Clayton take U.S. Hwy. 441 north for three miles into Mountain City. Turn left onto Black Rock Mountain Parkway and drive 2 miles up the mountain. Follow the signs to the park campground. The Ada-hi Falls trailhead is located on the left across from the campground store.

Trail and description

Ada-hi Falls is probably the smallest cascade listed in this entire guide, but it's still falling water and it's actually a nice scenic spot to visit. You may think *Ada-hi* is a Cherokee word for *tiny waterfall* but it actually means *forest*. This small cascade is perched high on the eastern slopes of lofty Black Rock Mountain, home of Georgia's highest state park. In fact, the cascade is so high on the mountain that Taylor Creek doesn't have a great deal of raw material to work with. Whatever water finds its way into the creek drips and splashes down a steep cliff face adjacent to a well-placed observation deck.

Though the path is only a few hundred yards there is an elevation change of several hundred feet. You'll get a quick workout as you descend the moderately steep path which includes several sets of steps. Be sure to visit the park's visitor center and its magnificent overlooks while you're here. Black Rock Mountain State Park is one of Georgia's most beautiful parks, and the views from the summit are exceptional.

Georgia Hub #7 - Northeast Rabun County

Rabun County's wonderful assortment of waterfalls continues with ten waterfalls in the northeastern quadrant of the county. This portion of Rabun County is Chattooga country - in fact the entire eastern border of the county is the incomparable Chattooga Wild and Scenic River. Famous for its world-renowned whitewater and infamous for its starring role in the 1970's film Deliverance, the river is one of the crown jewels of North American whitewater. Several waterfalls in this hub are found along this magnificent waterway.

Another notable landmark is Rabun Bald, Georgia's highest peak which checks in at a lofty 4,696 feet above sea level. Several trails lead to the top of this undeveloped peak, including the popular Bartram Trail which enters from North Carolina a few miles north of the mountain and passes two of our falls as it winds south through Warwoman Dell before turning east and intersecting the river near Sandy Ford and yet another waterfall - Dick's Creek Falls.

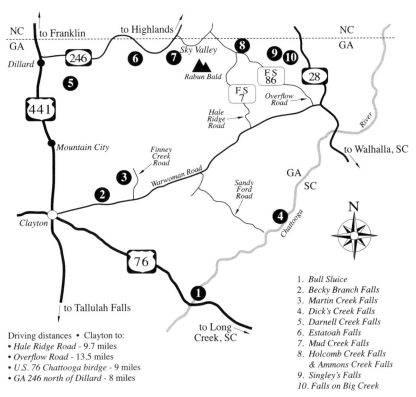

Driving distances • Clayton to:
• Hale Ridge Road - 9.7 miles
• Overflow Road - 13.5 miles
• U.S. 76 Chattooga birdge - 9 miles
• GA 246 north of Dillard - 8 miles

1. Bull Sluice
2. Becky Branch Falls
3. Martin Creek Falls
4. Dick's Creek Falls
5. Darnell Creek Falls
6. Estatoah Falls
7. Mud Creek Falls
8. Holcomb Creek Falls
   & Ammons Creek Falls
9. Singley's Falls
10. Falls on Big Creek

Bull Sluice

Stream: Chattooga River
Rating: excellent
Type: cascade
Height: 10 feet
Stream flow: large

USGS Quad: Rainy Mountain, GA, SC
Landowner: Chattooga Wild & Scenic River
Trail length: 250 yards (one way)
Difficulty: easy
Elevation: 1,210 feet

Directions

From Clayton take U.S. 76 east for 9 miles to the Chattooga River bridge. Cross the bridge and turn left into the day use parking area. The trail to Bull Sluice begins around the left side of the rest room/changing room area next to the river information board.

Bull Sluice from the South Carolina overlook

Description

Waterfall "purists" may scoff at the inclusion of Bull Sluice but this seething Class IV-V rapid on the Chattooga River is a vivid example of the raw power of moving water. You'll hear it long before you see it, and at high water you'll probably wonder why anyone would want to go through it in a tiny boat.

There are paths on both the Georgia and South Carolina sides of the river, but the South Carolina path is the only easy way to see the Bull in action. Follow the paved path downhill from the parking area and veer to the right onto a nicely graded gravel trail that leads a few hundred yards up to an observation point above the rapid. This area is a popular swimming hole and the rocks above the rapid make a great spot to take in the scene, but be very careful: they are steep and slippery, and the current here is extremely powerful. There have been numerous deaths in and around Bull Sluice over the years.

Becky Branch Falls

Stream: Becky Branch   USGS Quad: Rabun Bald, GA, NC
Rating: good   Landowner: Warwoman WMA
Type: cascade   Trail length: 0.25 mile (one way)
Height: 20 feet   Difficulty: moderate (steep uphill)
Stream flow: small   Elevation: 2,140 feet

Directions

From U.S. 441 in Clayton turn east onto Warwoman Road (next to the Days Inn) and proceed 2.4 miles to Warwoman Dell Recreation Area on the right. Park in the first small parking area on the left.

Trail and description

From the parking area walk west along the main road and locate the Bartram Trail's signature yellow markers. Turn right and take the trail past the old Civilian Conservation Corps trout holding pens; after a short ascent you'll cross Warwoman Road and enter the woods on the north side of the road. Continue up a moderately steep grade for a few hundred yards to a small footbridge just a few yards below the tiny cascade.

Becky Branch is very typical of the hundreds of small cascades that occur high in the watershed of local streams. At normal levels the cascade is noisy and playful as it splashes down the rock wall and disappears into a steep, narrow ravine; during dry spells it loses most of its charm.

Becky Branch Falls

Martin Creek Falls ★

Stream: Martin Creek
Rating: excellent
Type: cascade
Height: 40 feet
Stream flow: small

USGS Quad: Rabun Bald, GA, NC
Landowner: Warwoman WMA
Trail length: 0.5 mile (one way)
Difficulty: moderate
Elevation: 2,035 feet

Directions

From U.S. 441 in Clayton turn east onto Warwoman Road (next to the Days Inn) and proceed 3.1 miles to Finney Creek Road (FS 152) on the left. Drive 0.5 mile to a primitive camping area on the left and park here.

Trail and description

If you don't mind a few hundred yards of "social trail" you'll survive this unofficial route to Martin Creek Falls. From the primitive camping area look for the narrow path (sometimes flagged) that leads away from the road and into the woods. Rock hop across Martin Creek, then follow a shortcut path uphill for several hundred yards to the Bartram Trail. Veer right and continue 0.25 mile to the waterfall.

Initially the Bartram Trail follows alongside a dramatic ravine carved into the bedrock by Martin Creek. The creek dives over a series of ledges punctuated with impressive swirl holes. It's tough (and dangerous) to view, but a few highlights are visible. The trail then enters a broad expanse of open woods before crossing Martin Creek on a footbridge downstream of the falls.

Since Martin Creek Falls is located along the Bartram Trail you can also park at Warwoman Dell and walk the trail past Becky Branch Falls all the way to Martin Creek Falls. One way hiking time should be a little less than an hour, with an estimated distance of about 2.5 miles.

Martin Creek Falls

Dick's Creek Falls

Stream: Dick's Creek
Rating: excellent
Type: steep waterslide
Height: 50 feet
Stream flow: medium

USGS Quad: Satolah/Rainy Mountain, GA, SC
Landowner: Chattooga Wild & Scenic River
Trail length: 0.5 mile (one way)
Difficulty: easy
Elevation: 1,500 feet

Directions

From U.S. 441 in Clayton turn east onto Warwoman Road (next to the Days Inn) and proceed 5.6 miles. Turn right onto Sandy Ford Road. Proceed through an initial sharp right turn and drive 0.65 mile to the point where Sandy Ford Road turns abruptly left and crosses Warwoman Creek. Proceed 4 miles along the gravel road to the point where the road fords Dick's Creek. There is a small pull-off on the left preceding the ford. Park here.

Dick's Creek Falls

Trail and description

There are two ways to reach Dick's Creek Falls. The slightly shorter route described here utilizes an unmarked social trail. From the pull-off preceding Dick's Creek enter the woods and follow the trail along an old roadbed roughly paralleling the creek. At mile 0.4 the trail crosses the Bartram Trail, passes over a footbridge, then closely follows Dick's Creek downstream for several hundred yards to the brink of the cascade.

Alternate route: If you prefer to stay on an "official" trail, drive *through* Dick's Creek at the 4.0 mile point on Sandy Ford Road and continue 0.3 mile to the point where the Bartram Trail crosses the road. A large boulder on the right of the road marks the spot. Park in one of the primitive clearings on the left side of the road, then head east on the Bartram Trail. Walk several hundred yards and the Chattooga River Trail merges from the south. Spring displays of trillium and other wildflowers are especially good along this portion of the trail. Continue ahead for 0.5 mile and the trail comes alongside Dick's Creek. Turn right onto the old logging road that follows Dick's Creek several hundred yards downstream to the top of the cascade.

Dick's Creek Falls (also known as Five Finger Falls) tumbles gracefully into the Chattooga River above a dramatic bend in the river. A massive rock barrier known as Dick's Creek ledge actually blocks the river; several breaks in the ledge create a powerful Class IV whitewater rapid about mid-river. The combination of the river, the ledge and the waterfall creates a magnificently unique wilderness scene.

Because it is a wilderness cascade, be particularly careful around the deceptively slippery brink of the waterfall. The trail continues downhill to a point alongside the river-wide ledge. Several scramble paths drop steeply down the hillside to a vantage point at the base of the waterfall. It's beautiful, it's wild and it's dangerous, but this is a wonderful spot to witness the Chattooga's unmatched beauty. For an undeveloped waterfall it can also become a bit crowded. Plan your visit wisely and treat this area with respect.

Darnell Creek Falls

Stream: Darnell Creek
Rating: excellent
Type: cascade
Height: 30 feet
Stream flow: medium

USGS Quad: Rabun Bald, GA, NC
Landowner: Chattahoochee National Forest
Trail length: 200 yards (one way)
Difficulty: easy
Elevation: 2,300 feet

Directions

From Clayton take U.S. 441 north for 5.8 miles. Turn right onto Kelly's Creek Road at the traffic light (at the Rabun Gap Post Office). Proceed one mile and turn right onto Darnell Creek Road. Drive 0.5 mile and bear left at the fork with Chestnut Mountain Road. Continue on the gravel road for 0.25 mile to the point where a primitive road forks to the right and drops toward the creek. Park here and walk 200 yards upstream to the cascade.

Description

Darnell Creek Falls is a surprisingly energetic cascade just minutes from busy Hwy. 441 near Dillard and Rabun Gap. It's fairly easy to reach and requires a stroll of only a few hundred yards. The downside is that because you can literally drive up to it, the waterfall draws a good number of individuals who like to "party" and leave their trash behind. It's sad because this really is a beautiful cascade.

Darnell Creek roars down through a narrow cleft in the rock before pausing in a small plunge pool. The cascade cuts across a rugged cliff face that is largely exposed rock carpeted in lush green moss. The contrasts on the rock face are striking and present some excellent photo opportunities.

Darnell Creek Falls

Estatoah Falls

Stream: Mud Creek
Rating: excellent
Type: steep cascade
Height: several hundred feet
Stream flow: medium

USGS Quad: Rabun Bald, GA, NC
Landowner: private property
Trail length: roadside view
Difficulty: n/a
Elevation: 2,500 feet

Directions

From Clayton take U.S. 441 north for approximately 8 miles. Proceed through Dillard then turn right onto GA 246. Proceed one mile and the lower portions of the cascade become visible low on the mountainside ahead. Estatoah is particularly impressive after heavy rains when the entire exposed cliff face is consumed with a graceful veil of falling water. There is no public access to the base of the waterfall, so enjoy the long range view from the highway.

Mud Creek Falls ★

Stream: Mud Creek	USGS Quad: Rabun Bald, GA, NC
Rating: excellent	Landowner: Sky Valley Resort
Type: cascade	Trail length: roadside
Height: 60 feet	Difficulty: n/a
Stream flow: medium	Elevation: 2,980 feet

Directions

From Clayton take U.S. 441 north for approximately 8 miles. Continue through Dillard then turn right onto GA 246. Drive 4.2 miles then turn right onto Bald Mountain Road at the Sinclair station/country store. Proceed 0.9 mile to the Sky Valley entrance and turn right. After passing the gate turn left and drive 0.5 mile to Tahoe Lane on the right. Follow Tahoe Lane for 0.75 mile to the base of the cascade and park.

Mud Creek Falls

Description

This beautiful waterfall simply deserves a better name. Though Mud Creek Falls and Estatoah Falls share the same stream, they offer up dramatically different waterfall experiences. While Estatoah must be admired from afar, you can practically reach out and touch beautiful Mud Creek Falls. The cascade literally leaps from the upper cliff face and features several powerful roostertails about mid-way down the drop. The stream then rushes past a small picnic area at the base of the falls. The uppermost drops of the cascade are nearly vertical, while the last ten feet or so tumble over a scenic set of frothing shoals. Please respect this private property and be on your best behavior.

Holcomb Creek Falls & Ammons Falls ★

Stream: Holcomb Creek   USGS Quad: Rabun Bald, GA, NC
Rating: excellent   Landowner: Chattahoochee National Forest
Type: cascade   Trail length: 0.5 mile (one way)
Height: 125 feet   Difficulty: moderate (elevation change)
Stream flow: small   Elevation: 2,440 feet

Directions

From U.S. 441 in Clayton turn east onto Warwoman Road (next to the Days Inn) and proceed 9.7 miles to Hale Ridge Road (FS 7) on the left. Follow Hale Ridge Road for 6.6 miles to the intersection of Hale Ridge Road and Overflow Road (FS 86). Park here. The trail (#52) begins on the north side of the intersection.

If you are driving to the falls from the Sky Valley area, continue on Bald Mountain Road past the Sky Valley entrance approximately 3 miles until you reach Hale Ridge Road on the right. Follow Hale Ridge Road down to the intersection of Hale Ridge Road and Overflow Road (drive time approximately 10 minutes).

Trail and description

Water flow can make or break the beauty of Holcomb Creek Falls. When the creek is full it is one of the most scenic waterfalls in northeast Georgia. When the water drops, not so much. In my last 3 visits to Holcomb I had hoped to catch the waterfall "booming" but became so frustrated that I decided not to include a photo. They simply did not do justice to the falls.

This beauty stairsteps over an upper and middle ledge before cascading over a sloped rock face then regrouping in the creek bed below. A large boulder pile along the right side of the cascade's base is an inviting observation point, but take it from one who knows - the rocks are very slippery. I fell here years ago and effectively ruined an expensive camera lens. Please heed the warning signs and stay off the waterfall.

Continue along the pathway past Holcomb Creek Falls. The trail begins to climb moderately for several hundred yards and you will soon notice the sounds of yet another stream to the right. Continue climbing and shortly after passing a spur trail on your left the trail ends at a large observation platform just a few feet from splashing **Ammons Creek Falls** (also known as Emory Branch Falls). Ammons Creek Falls is a fairly minor 40-foot cascade but it is definitely worth a look if you are here to see Holcomb Creek Falls.

Alternate route: Visitors to these two waterfalls may choose to retrace their steps to the parking area or they can choose to lengthen their hike by taking the spur trail that begins below Ammons Creek Falls. This trail closely follows splashing Holcomb Creek for one mile upstream (*note: uphill*) to an alternate trailhead along Hale Ridge Road (FS 7). This portion of Holcomb Creek features dozens of small shoals and a few notable cascades. This upper trailhead is 0.6 mile north of the original trailhead at the FS 7/FS 86 junction. Exit the woods and turn left and you'll be back at your car in about ten minutes. Add it all up and you have a delightfully challenging 2.1 mile loop.

*Ammons
Creek Falls*

Falls on Big Creek

Stream: Big Creek   USGS Quad: Satolah, GA, NC
Rating: excellent   Landowner: Chattahoochee National Forest
Type: cascade   Trail length: 2.0 miles (one way)
Height: 50 feet   Difficulty: difficult
Stream flow: large   Elevation: 2,250 feet

Directions

From U.S. 441 in Clayton, turn east onto Warwoman Road (next to the Days Inn) and proceed 14 miles to Hwy 28. Turn left and drive 4.5 miles to the community of Satolah. Cross the bridge over Big Creek, then proceed several hundred feet and turn left into a primitive parking area. There is an old logging road that crosses Talley Mill Creek adjacent to the parking area. The hike begins here.

Trail and description

The imaginatively named Big Creek features a highly scenic cascade that is a very worthy destination for adventurous waterfall lovers. This one might become a major attraction if it were just easier to access. All the elements come together here to create a very special waterfall: lots of stream flow, a sizable drop, huge streamside boulders, bare rock walls and lush vegetation. The obstacles include: it is remote, there is no maintained or signed trail, and what trail there is just about disappears around the waterfall. Other than that, piece of cake!

Falls on Big Creek

From the parking area along Hwy. 28 in Satolah step across Talley Mill Creek and begin walking along the old road bed. Walk along the fairly gentle grade for 1.5 miles to the point where a side trail intersects from the left. The trail straight ahead continues to Three Forks and to Singley's Falls on Overflow Creek. To reach the falls on Big Creek, turn left and begin a gentle descent to the creek. After 0.5 mile the trail reaches Big Creek and bends right as it follows the creek downstream.

The trail becomes rougher and less defined as you near the vicinity of the falls. Using caution, locate the side path that leads to the base and descend very carefully down the steep and slippery bank to the plunge pool. There is a nice view of the final cascade from this area and a fairly respectable area of bedrock along the edge of the stream makes a nice vantage point. The entire volume of Big Creek is squeezed into a narrow fluming drop that plunges over a series of upper cascades somewhat obscured from view before vaulting into the deep plunge pool in one final powerful drop.

Singley's Falls

Stream: Overflow Creek
Rating: excellent
Type: cascade
Height: 15 feet
Stream flow: large

USGS Quad: Satolah, GA, NC
Landowner: Chattooga Wild & Scenic River
Trail length: 3.2 miles (one way)
Difficulty: difficult (elevation change)
Elevation: 2,010 feet

Directions

From U.S. 441 in Clayton turn east onto Warwoman Road (next to the Days Inn) and proceed 14 miles to Hwy 28. Turn left and drive 4.5 miles to the community of Satolah. Cross the bridge over Big Creek, then proceed several hundred feet and turn left into a primitive parking area. There is an old logging road that crosses Talley Mill Creek adjacent to the parking area. The hike begins here.

Trail and description

The hike to Singley's Falls on Overflow Creek is long and strenuous. It is definitely not for children or individuals who are not physically fit. Consider yourself warned. For those who make it however, you'll get to experience a powerful and stunningly beautiful cascade. Overflow Creek is a West Fork Chattooga River tributary that plummets through beautiful Blue

Valley before merging with Big Creek and Holcomb Creek at Three Forks.

To reach the falls wade or rock hop across Talley Mill Creek and begin your walk down the old logging road. At mile 1.5 pass a side trail to the left that descends to the falls on Big Creek, 0.6 mile distant. Continue another 0.9 mile along a fairly easy grade until mile 2.4 when you arrive at a vehicle-blocking mound of dirt with a large open pit (normally holding a good bit of water). The trail to Singley's Falls is to the right. The trail wastes no time as it begins to descend into the Overflow Creek gorge.

Continue for 0.6 mile to a point where the trail turns sharply right. At this point locate the narrow path to the left that descends about 0.2 mile down to the top of the falls. A side path runs down the left side of the falls to the base. This beautiful cascade begins as a series of cascades that funnel inward into one powerful chute. The deep green pool at the base is known as "eel pool" and is both expansive and deep. The cascade is perfectly framed between the massive shoulders of dark streamside rocks and lush vegetation. This is a wonderful spot to linger. Use caution and good sense here - Singley's Falls is isolated and potentially dangerous, and it would take a long time to get help if an injury occurred.

Singley's Falls
Overflow Creek

Georgia Hub #8 - Cohutta Wilderness

Several of Georgia's most beautiful waterfalls are located in this section of north central and northwest Georgia that's a bit out of the state's traditional waterfall belt. The mountains in northwest Georgia are very different from those of northeast Georgia. While northeast Georgia mountains are part of the Blue Ridge geologic region, those in the northwestern corner are part of the Appalachian Plateau region. The two are separated by the Valley and Ridge region, a great fault that stretches northeast well into Pennsylvania.

It makes for fascinating reading but what it really means to waterfall lovers is that the mountains in the northwestern corner have retained sedimentary features uncommon to those in northeast Georgia. Some of the falls in the northwestern corner, such as those in Cloudland Canyon State Park and in the Lula Land Trust are free falling waterfalls rarely seen in the northeastern corner of the state. In this edition I have included major falls as far west as the edge of the Blue Ridge region; those of northwest Georgia will come in the next edition. For now, only one waterfall is detailed, and it's one of the largest by volume in the state: Jack's River Falls in the Cohutta Wilderness.

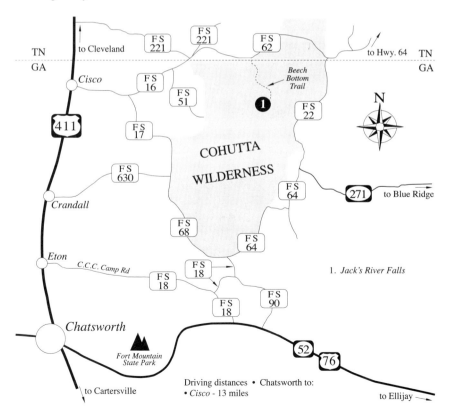

1. *Jack's River Falls*

Driving distances • Chatsworth to:
• *Cisco* - 13 miles

Jack's River Falls

Stream: Jack's River
Rating: excellent
Type: cascade/free-fall
Height: 50 feet
Stream flow: large

USGS Quad: Hemp Top, GA, TN
Landowner: Cohutta Wilderness
Trail length: 4.5 miles (one way)
Difficulty: moderate to difficult
Elevation: 1,540 feet

Directions

From Chatsworth take Hwy. 411 north for 13 miles to Cisco. Turn right onto Old GA 2 / FS 16 right before the Cisco Baptist Church. Proceed 10 miles (only the first 1.8 miles are paved) to FS 62. Turn right on FS 62 and drive 4.4 miles to the Jack's River trailhead.

Quick history

The Cohutta Wilderness consists of nearly 37,000 acres of National Forest land in North Georgia and Tennessee that has been set aside since 1975 to remain undisturbed, but this was not always the case. In one of North Georgia's great enterprises of the early twentieth century nearly 70 percent of this area was logged. From 1915 into the 1930s hundreds of workers were employed by the Conasauga River Lumber Company which operated logging railroads along both the Jacks and Conasauga Rivers. Today the loggers are gone and the area has returned to its natural state.

Trail and description

The Cohutta Wilderness has long been a favorite of Georgia hikers, and one of this area's best known trails leads to a Cohutta favorite - Jacks River Falls. The shortest and most popular route to Jacks River Falls is along the

Jack's River Falls

Beech Bottom Trail. This 4.0 mile trail connects the northern access road (which is partially in Tennessee) with the Jacks River. The trail follows an old road generally southeast through the northern part of the wilderness. The path features a delightfully gentle grade with only minor ups or downs through most of the hike. A moderate descent occurs as the trail drops into Beech Bottoms. The path turns nearly due south and winds through the bottoms for 0.5 mile to an intersection with Jacks River Trail at mile 4.0. Turn right and follow the river *downstream* for 0.5 mile to the top of rugged Jacks River Falls.

Anytime you venture into a wilderness area you need to have a current copy of the area's trail map system with you. This trail description has been purposely oversimplified and does not intend to take the place of a detailed map. There are many trails that lace the Cohutta Wilderness and the intersections can be confusing. Always let someone know where you are and be prepared for the unexpected.

Waterfall description

This beautiful waterfall crashes through some of the most rugged terrain in North Georgia. Some sources claim that Jacks River Falls has the highest average water flow of any Georgia waterfall; what this means to you is that it usually has lots of water. The main cascade is about 50 feet high but add the long shoals above the falls and it means lots of action. The area above the falls attracts large crowds of waders, swimmers, and sunbathers. Some visitors cannot resist the urge and jump from the high rocks on the opposite side of the river into a deep swimming hole. This area receives a great deal of visitation in the summer.

The waterfall can be viewed from above as the trail passes but to really explore the scene you must descend a steep, slippery scramble path littered with loose rock to the riverbed below the falls. To be safe you'll need to use your hands.

Section II

northwestern
South Carolina

South Carolina Hub #1 - Long Creek

Oconee County, South Carolina, features a surprisingly large number of excellent waterfalls. Nearly all lie in the western end of the county in either the Chattooga River or Chauga River watersheds. Both Oconee County hubs featured in this book feature a tremendous variety of waterfalls as well. From the beautiful cascades on tiny streams such as Opossum Creek and Reedy Branch to the thundering waters of the Chattooga's Big Bend Falls and Lower Whitewater Falls on the spectacular Whitewater River, Oconee County takes a back seat to no one when it comes to falling water.

You may have come for the waterfalls but this part of upstate South Carolina is Chattooga River country. Whitewater boating is king, and hiking, camping and fishing are right behind. Trout fishing in particular is quite popular on many of the river's feeder streams. You'll quickly notice that the Long Creek area is at the core (couldn't resist) for the apple business as well, with dozens of lush orchards along the highways and backroads of the area.

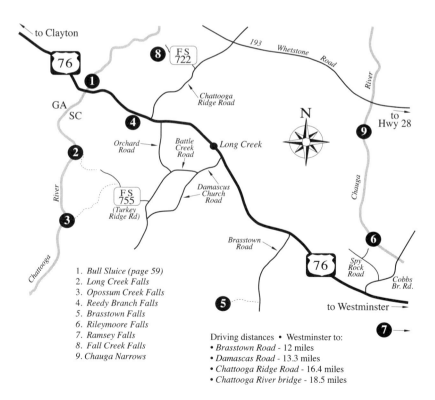

1. Bull Sluice (page 59)
2. Long Creek Falls
3. Opossum Creek Falls
4. Reedy Branch Falls
5. Brasstown Falls
6. Rileymoore Falls
7. Ramsey Falls
8. Fall Creek Falls
9. Chauga Narrows

Driving distances • Westminster to:
• Brasstown Road - 12 miles
• Damascas Road - 13.3 miles
• Chattooga Ridge Road - 16.4 miles
• Chattooga River bridge - 18.5 miles

Long Creek Falls ★

Stream: Long Creek
Rating: excellent
Type: cascade
Height: 30 feet
Stream flow: medium

USGS Quad: Rainy Mountain, GA, SC
Landowner: Chattooga Wild & Scenic River
Trail length: 1.6 miles (one way)
Difficulty: moderate (steep final descent)
Elevation: 1,080 feet

Directions

From Westminster proceed west on U.S. 76 for 13.3 miles. Turn left onto Damascus Church Road. Proceed 0.9 mile and turn right onto Battle Creek Road (SC-102). Proceed 1.9 miles to FS 755 (Turkey Ridge Road) on the right. Follow FS 755 for 3 miles to a large gravel parking area. Note: 4-WD vehicles may follow the primitive road to the right of the parking area for an additional 0.6 mile to an alternate parking area. This final 0.6 mile is very rough and features several enormous pools of water in the road.

If you are coming from Rabun County follow U.S. 76 from the Chattooga River bridge for 4.7 miles to Damascus Church Road on the right.

*Late summer brings
low water to Long
Creek Falls*

Description
Undoubtedly more whitewater boaters see beautiful Long Creek Falls than do hikers. This impressive cascade is a mandatory stopping point for boaters as they test the thundering whitewater of the Chattooga River's daunting Section IV. This wide crashing 30-foot drop splits into several distinct tongues as it descends into a picturesque cove just a few hundred feet from its confluence with the Chattooga.

Trail description
The route to the falls begins at a large parking turnaround on FS 755 about 3 miles from Battle Creek Road. Assuming you don't try to drive any further (good idea) begin walking along the old logging road that begins on the right side of the parking area. Follow it for 0.6 mile (stay right where it forks to the left) to a small clearing where the road ends.

On the right side of the clearing follow the trail into the woods beyond a vehicle-blocking mound. A Chattooga River boundary marker just beyond the clearing will assure you that you are on the right trail. The trail follows an old logging road for approximately one mile. The grade is fairly gentle but the trail can become a bit overgrown in the summer months. Beyond the half mile point the trail gently loops into several west-facing coves as it heads north now paralleling the Chattooga River.

At about the 1 mile point (1.6 miles from the first parking area), a prominent side trail to the left drops steeply toward the river. As of my last visit, a large pile of sticks and limbs blocks the main trail and directs you onto the side trail. I have also seen the side trail marked with surveying tape. The side trail drops steeply through a thick grove of laurel for just over 100 yards before passing the upper cascades of Long Creek Falls on the right. The path terminates at the point where Long Creek flows into the Chattooga River. Wade or rock-hop across Long Creek (mandatory to get up close - keep this in mind if planning a winter hike) and follow the well-defined path on the north bank of the creek to several excellent vantage points.

If you linger here for any amount of time you're sure to see rafters and kayakers float by. You may even have company as whitewater outfitters and private boaters have made Long Creek Falls a favorite lunch spot. Many visitors venture out onto the rocks below the left tongue and take an icy shower under the cascade. While I never recommend this because of the obvious dangers that occur when water meets rock, many people take the risk. Try to avoid the temptation to venture to the top of the waterfall. It's simply too dangerous and you're a long way from help if anything bad were to occur.

Opossum Creek Falls

Stream: Opossum Creek   USGS Quad: Rainy Mountain, GA,SC
Rating: excellent   Landowner: Chattooga Wild & Scenic River
Type: cascade   Trail length: 2.5 miles (one way)
Height: 75 feet   Difficulty: strenuous (elevation change)
Stream flow: small   Elevation: 1,050 feet

Directions

From Westminster proceed west on U.S. 76 for 13.3 miles. Turn left onto Damascus Church Road. Proceed 0.9 mile and turn right onto Battle Creek Road (SC-102). Proceed 1.9 miles to FS 755 (Turkey Ridge Road) on the right. Follow FS 755 for 2.2 miles to FS 755-F on the left. Park in one of the pull-offs along the side of the road and walk back along FS 755 for about 50 yards to the trailhead on the right. If you are coming from Rabun County, follow U.S. 76 from the Chattooga River bridge for 4.7 miles to Damascus Church Road on the right.

Description

The Opossum Creek Trail was completely relocated following a destructive tornado in the spring of 1994. The trail was moved west of its original location because literally hundreds of fallen trees made the path impossible to negotiate. The new and improved Opossum Creek Trail actually follows tiny Camp Branch for most of its splashing journey down to the Chattooga River just downstream of the infamous Five Falls section.

This hike is not to be taken lightly. Though it comes in at 5 miles round trip, there is a deceptive loss in elevation on the way in. Common sense tells you that what goes down must eventually come back up, and the return hike is fairly strenuous (particularly the first mile after you leave the river on the way out). Only a few short stretches actually rate as steep, but the grade is fairly relentless. Don't attempt it if you are not accustomed to long hikes. The 2.2 mile stretch from the parking area to the river is quite scenic with a constantly changing parade of ferns and ground covers such as galax lining the heavily forested route into the protected Chattooga River corridor.

Visitors will hear the roar of the river long before arriving at the point where Opossum Creek's waters mingle with the Chattooga. Be sure to make your way to the riverbank where you can often catch whitewater boaters floating by as they near the end of rugged Section IV. A spur trail leads from here upstream to Opossum Creek Falls. The trail begins at a marker in a primitive camping area alongside the river and creek. Follow the well-defined but rough trail for 0.3 mile crossing two small branches along the way.

The spur trail ends at a rock garden just below the lower drops of Opossum Creek Falls. Climb over and around the rocks until you reach a nice vantage point just downstream of the lower cascades which drop about 50 feet. The uppermost cascades are clearly visible high above the main drop but they are set back so that it is difficult to tell just how high this waterfall really is. My estimate is that the total series of cascades is perhaps 150 feet.

Opossum Creek Falls

Reedy Branch Falls

Stream: Reedy Branch
Rating: good
Type: cascade
Height: 30 feet
Stream flow: small

USGS Quad: Rainy Mountain, GA, SC
Landowner: Sumter National Forest
Trail length: 250 yards (one way)
Difficulty: easy
Elevation: approx. 1,600 feet

Directions

From Westminster proceed west on U.S. 76 for 16.8 miles. Turn left at a gravel road on the left with a stacked stone wall and gate. There is a Forest Service road marker which denotes FS 2751. Park here being careful not to block the gate. (This point is just beyond the junction of Hwy. 76 and Chattooga Ridge Road. If you are coming from Rabun County, follow Hwy. 76 from the Chattooga River bridge for 1.9 miles to FS 2751 on the right.

Description

The pretty cascade on Reedy Branch is one of the easiest waterfalls in this book to access. From the parking area along U.S. 76 walk down a gravel road for several hundred yards to the point where Reedy Branch flows under the road. Look for the prominent trail on the left side of the road leading into the woods. Walk about 50 yards to the base of this scenic cascade which tumbles over a broken cliff of dark moss-covered rocks. Seasonal wildflowers proliferate the open area in front of the tiny plunge pool, and the shallow stream provides several nice vantage points for photography. Reedy Branch is fairly small, so the waterfall doesn't offer a lot during dry periods. Catch it after a heavy rain and it nearly covers the cliff face.

Falls on Reedy Branch

Falls on Brasstown Creek ★

Directions

From Westminster proceed west on U.S. 76 for 12 miles and turn left onto Brasstown Road (S-48). Proceed 2.7 miles. At this point the pavement ends. Continue an additional 1.5 miles to FS 751 on the right. Follow FS 751 to the small parking area at the end of the road. Park here.

Description

Brasstown Falls is actually a series of three very different waterfalls which occur back-to-back-to-back just a short walk from the parking area. There are a few drawbacks to Brasstown though. The ease of access leads to large numbers of visitors and the area around the falls can become a bit trashy. Several primitive campsites just above the first waterfall detract somewhat from solitude you might be seeking. Also, the "trail" to the lower two waterfalls leaves a lot to be desired. It is very steep, slippery and requires a free hand to use roots and limbs for hand holds. If you don't mind the obstacles and crowds don't bother you it is quite simply a fantastic stretch of creek.

Brasstown #1 - Brasstown Cascades

Stream: Brasstown Creek
Rating: excellent
Type: cascade
Height: 40 feet
Stream flow: medium

USGS Quad: Tugaloo Lake, GA, SC
Landowner: Sumter National Forest
Trail length: 0.2 mile (one way)
Difficulty: moderate
Elevation: approx. 1,000 feet

Description

The first waterfall encountered is just a few hundred yards from the parking area at the end of FS 751. This pretty 30-foot drop is commonly referred to as Brasstown Cascades, or Upper Brasstown Falls. Here Brasstown Creek stairsteps over a wide open ledge. Viewing the waterfall is quite easy from a number of streamside locations.

Brasstown Veil
as seen from the path
- description on next page

Brasstown #2 - Brasstown Veil ★

Stream: Brasstown Creek
Rating: excellent
Type: free-fall
Height: 30 feet
Stream flow: medium

USGS Quad: Tugaloo Lake, GA, SC
Landowner: Sumter National Forest
Trail length: additional 50 yards
Difficulty: moderate with hazards
Elevation: approx. 960 feet

Trail and description

A short series of low ledges separates Brasstown Cascades from the next waterfall just downstream. This beautiful drop is known as Brasstown Veil and once you see it you'll know why. Brasstown Veil is formed as the creek separates into two distinct tongues and drops over a sheer river-wide ledge. As you negotiate the steep trail that connects Brasstown Cascades from Brasstown Veil you will pass a scenic vantage point that looks down on the drop from above (see photo on the previous page). It's tricky to brace yourself for a good photograph but it is one of the best vantage points for this beautiful waterfall. Continue down the trail to the base, being very careful to use roots and rocks to steady yourself. At the base you can look at the waterfall nearly straight on and get a nice view of the mesmerizing veil of falling water that stretches across the creek from bank to bank.

view of Brasstown Veil from the plunge pool

Brasstown #3 - Brasstown Sluice

Stream: Brasstown Creek
Rating: excellent
Type: steep waterslide
Height: 40 feet
Stream flow: medium

USGS Quad: Tugaloo Lake, GA, SC
Landowner: Sumter National Forest
Trail length: additional 50 yards
Difficulty: moderate with hazards
Elevation: approx. 920 feet

*Brassstown
Sluice*

Trail and description

Of the three waterfalls along Brasstown Creek, Brasstown Sluice is the farthest from the parking lot and definitely the trickiest to access. Regardless of the obstacles, everyone wants to enjoy the swimming hole/plunge pool below this narrow cascade. Brasstown Sluice surges through a cleft in the ledge before pausing in the broad plunge pool. A massive rock wall to the right of the sluice adds to the rugged beauty of this powerful drop. Portions of the cliff are covered with ferns and mosses creating a magnificent wilderness scene.

Note: Keep in mind that the paths to these waterfalls are really more like scramble paths and there are no railings or decks from which to safely view these three waterfalls. They are definitely not kid friendly, yet scores of children can be found here on any given summer day. Those not accustomed to steep climbs up slippery exposed slopes may want to skip the lower two waterfalls. Use extreme caution along these paths.

Rileymoore Falls

Stream: Chauga River   USGS Quad: Holly Springs, SC, GA
Rating: good   Landowner: Sumter National Forest
Type: steep cascade   Trail length: 1 mile (one way)
Height: 10-12 feet   Difficulty: moderate
Stream flow: large   Elevation: approx. 800 feet

Directions

From Westminster proceed west on U.S. 76 for 7.5 miles. Turn right onto Cobb Bridge Road (S-37) and proceed 1.4 miles to Spy Rock Road (FS 748) on the left. Proceed along FS 748 for 1.8 miles to FS 748C on the right. Park here along the side of the road. Follow FS 748C on foot for approximately 0.5 mile, bearing to the right when you come to the fork in the road. When you reach the Forest Service gate locate the trail to the left and follow it for about 0.7 mile to the waterfall.

Description

Although Rileymoore Falls checks in at a relatively small 12 feet, this river wide ledge is a very worthy waterfall. Located on the scenic Chauga River, Riley Moore Falls was once the location of a mill that served this portion of Oconee County. Today the ledge is known primarily as a challenging Class IV-V rapid that Chauga boaters must either run or portage. Rileymoore Falls tumbles over a broad ledge onto a large boulder pile creating a massive wall of roaring whitewater. A large pool at the base of the drop attracts swimmers in the hot summer months but the scenery at the falls is enjoyable in any season.

Ramsey Falls

Stream: Ramsey Creek   USCS Quad: Holly Springs, SC, GA
Rating: good   Landowner: Chau-Ram County Park
Type: steep cascade   Trail length: roadside
Height: 30 feet   Difficulty: easy
Stream flow: medium   Elevation: approx. 750 feet

Directions

From Westminster proceed west on U.S. 76 for 2.5 miles. Turn left into Chau-Ram County Park.

Description

      This pretty cascade tumbles over a broad broken ledge in several distinct cascades before spilling into the Chauga River just downstream of the Hwy. 76 bridge. Chau-Ram Park is a popular destination for picnickers and a put-in/take-out point for whitewater boaters on the Chauga River. Though it's a minor cascade, the park and river offer up some nice scenery.

Ramsey Falls

Falls on Fall Creek

Stream: Fall Creek   USGS Quad: Whetstone, GA, SC
Rating: excellent   Landowner: Sumter National Forest
Type: steep cascade   Trail length: 50 yards to first cascade
Height: 30 feet   Difficulty: moderate to difficult
Stream flow: small   Elevation: approx. 1,600 feet

Directions

      From Westminster proceed west on U.S. 76 for 16.4 miles. Turn right onto Chattooga Ridge Road (S-196) and proceed 2 miles to Fall Creek Road (FS 722) on the left. Proceed along Fall Creek Road for 0.3 mile. Turn left onto Fall Creek Extension and proceed 0.5 mile to the creek crossing. The only markings to note the crossing are vertical yellow signs with black diagonal stripes. There is a pull off beyond the bridge on the left.

Description

      Fall Creek is appropriately named as it tumbles continually on its journey to the Chattooga River north of Hwy. 76. The stretch of Fall Creek from Fall Creek Road to the Chattooga features 3 scenic waterfalls ranging in height from 20 feet to about 40 feet. One of these cascades is just a few hundred feet down a steep primitive trail at the pull off along Fall Creek

Road. This steep narrow cascade plunges into a shallow plunge pool deep within a hidden ravine.

The other two cascades downstream require fairly difficult hikes, largely because there is no developed or maintained trail. A primitive path snakes downstream, but it soon diminishes into a scramble among the thick streamside groves of laurel and rhododendron. Because of the rough terrain and thick undergrowth this journey is slow and deliberate and it's difficult to accurately gauge the distances you have walked.

The best estimates I have come up with are approximately 1 mile to middle falls (20 foot cascade) and 2 miles to the lower falls (beautiful multi-tiered 40 foot cascade). The lower cascade is just upstream of Fall Creek's confluence with the Chattooga River. Since there is no established trail, it is highly recommended that anyone attempting this hike have a good map or GPS and stay close to the stream to keep from getting disoriented. This is a fairly strenuous hike - allow a minimum of 3-4 hours for the total trip.

*upper cascade
on Fall Creek*

South Carolina Hub #2 - Northwest Oconee

Northwest Oconee County is a waterfall lover's paradise. A dozen outstanding waterfalls and cascades are featured in this hub and, with a few exceptions, most are reasonably short hikes. The difficulty levels for these hikes do have quite a range however. Be sure to read about each waterfall carefully before deciding whether you should attempt a visit.

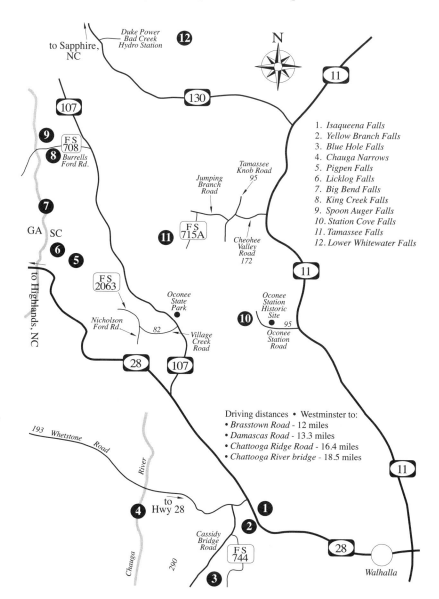

to Sapphire, NC

Duke Power Bad Creek Hydro Station

N

1. *Isaqueena Falls*
2. *Yellow Branch Falls*
3. *Blue Hole Falls*
4. *Chauga Narrows*
5. *Pigpen Falls*
6. *Licklog Falls*
7. *Big Bend Falls*
8. *King Creek Falls*
9. *Spoon Auger Falls*
10. *Station Cove Falls*
11. *Tamassee Falls*
12. *Lower Whitewater Falls*

FS 708
Burrells Ford Rd.

Tamassee Knob Road 95

Jumping Branch Road

GA SC

FS 715A

Cheohee Valley Road 172

FS 2063

Oconee State Park

Nicholson Ford Rd.

82

Village Creek Road

Oconee Station Historic Site

95
Oconee Station Road

28

107

to Highlands, NC

Chauga

193 Whetstone Road

River

Driving distances • Westminster to:
• *Brasstown Road* - 12 miles
• *Damascas Road* - 13.3 miles
• *Chattooga Ridge Road* - 16.4 miles
• *Chattooga River bridge* - 18.5 miles

to Hwy 28

Cassidy Bridge Road

FS 744

290

28

Walhalla

Issaqueena Falls

Stream: Cane Creek
Rating: excellent
Type: steep cascade
Height: 100 feet
Stream flow: small

USGS Quad: Walhalla, SC
Landowner: Stumphouse Tunnel Park
Trail length: 50 yards to overlook
Difficulty: easy to top/ difficult to bottom
Elevation: approx. 1,400 feet

Directions

From Walhalla, proceed west on Hwy. 28 for 6.9 miles. If you are coming from the north the park is located 0.7 mile south of the Hwy. 28/ Whetstone Road intersection. Turn right into Stumphouse Tunnel Park. Follow the road downhill for 0.4 mile to the picnic area on the right.

Issaqueena Falls

Trail and description

Issaqueena Falls, named after a Choctaw princess that legend has it was in love with an English trader, is one of the easiest of Oconee County's waterfalls to visit and view. From the creekside picnic area follow the level path across the footbridge past the brink of the waterfall and out to a large wooden observation platform. This vantage point looks back toward the parking area toward the top of the pretty cascade. This walk offers up a nice south facing view of the countryside as well.

An even better view of the falls can be obtained by descending along a steep, primitive trail from the deck to the boulder-strewn base of the first series of drops. The view from here is somewhat reminiscent of nearby Yellow Branch Falls as Issaqeena's waters spread across the wide rock face and mingle downward in narrow chutes and channels. Issaqueena is much more impressive after moderate to heavy rains as the flow dominates the cliff face with tumbling water. Be forewarned: the primitive path that drops to the lower viewing area is steep, slippery and often somewhat muddy. It is not for small children or those not in good shape. An even worse "path" continues from this spot to a lower tier of drops but this path is definitely not recommended. It is even steeper and could be categorized as treacherous.

Historical note

Ancient legend has it that Choctaw Princess Issaqueena was in love with Allan Francis, an English trader. Cherokee chief Kuruga disapproved of the relationship and the story goes that Kuruga forced Issaqueena to renounce the trader. When Issaqueena learned of Kuruga's plan to kill the Englishman, she fled camp at nearby Keowee and journeyed to warn the colony. Legend has it that Kuruga pursued Issaqeena to this high waterfall where Kuruga believed Issaqueena had leapt to her death. For the romantically inclined, an alternate version has Issaqueena hiding below the brink of the falls and continuing on in her journey until she successfully warned the colony and ultimately married Francis. The end.

On yet another historical note be sure to visit the nearby Stumphouse tunnel during your visit to the park. Began in the 1850s as a part of the failed Blue Ridge Railroad venture, the uncompleted tunnel was part of a grand scheme to link Walhalla and the region east of the Blue Ridge with the Tennessee Valley to the north and west. Approximately 1,600 feet of the tunnel was completed before the project was shut down due in part to conditions brought on by the Civil War in the early 1860s. A portion of the tunnel collapsed in 1990. The city of Walhalla, which operates the park, is considering plans that could reopen at least a portion of the tunnel to visitors.

Yellow Branch Falls ★

Stream: Yellow Branch
Rating: excellent
Type: steep cascade
Height: 60 feet
Stream flow: small

USGS Quad: Walhalla, SC
Landowner: Sumter National Forest
Trail length: 1.5 miles (one way)
Difficulty: moderate
Elevation: approx. 1,280 feet

Directions

From Walhalla proceed west on Hwy. 28 for 6.8 miles. Turn left into the Yellow Branch Picnic Area and proceed to the parking area.

Trail and description

In my opinion Yellow Branch Falls is one of the most scenic small stream waterfalls in the Blue Ridge. A mushroom-shaped rock at the brink of the falls directs the stream flow all across the dark rock face, creating an intricate maze of cascading water. It's very pretty even at low water as dozens of drips spill across the cliff, but when the water is up it is simply spellbinding. With luck, catch it after a summer thunderstorm and you'll be hooked forever on Yellow Branch Falls.

From the parking area locate the Yellow Branch Picnic Area information board just a stone's throw to the south. Begin your hike on the picnic area's Nature Trail. Follow this path for 0.2 mile downstream along small but scenic Yellow Branch. Turn right onto the Yellow Branch Falls Trail and continue along an undulating course through a beautiful forest setting for 1.3 miles to the base of the waterfall.

Yellow Branch Falls - low water of late summer

Blue Hole Falls

Stream: Cedar Creek
Rating: excellent
Type: steep waterslide
Height: 75 feet
Stream flow: medium

USGS Quadrangle: Whetstone, SC, GA
Landowner: Sumter National Forest
Trail length: 0.5 mile (one way)
Difficulty: difficult/dangerous (not for children)
Elevation: approx. 1,300 feet

Directions

From Walhalla proceed west on Hwy. 28 for just over 7 miles. Turn left onto Whetstone Road (S-193). Proceed west for 0.8 mile then turn left onto Cassidy Bridge Road (S-290). Drive 0.9 mile and turn left onto FS 744 (Rich Mountain Road). Proceed along this gravel road for 3.3 miles, then turn right onto FS 744C (Cedar Creek Road). Note: the last time I visited here FS 744C was unmarked. Proceed 2.5 miles on FS 744C to FS 2658 on the right. Park here.

Trail and description

This off-the-beaten-path waterfall is absolutely one of the wildest in the region. Blue Hole Falls possesses a few frustrating difficulties that may keep some people from visiting however. To begin with not everyone wants to drive nearly 6 miles on dirt roads just to reach the trailhead. This area is quite isolated so take this into account. Secondly, even though the walk is only about a half mile one way, it involves a wet crossing of a sizeable stream and then a tricky descent along a hazardous trail. Blue Hole Falls is a most worthy destination but it is not for small children or those afraid of heights.

From the parking area at the junction of FS 744C and FS 2658, walk downhill along FS 2658 for 0.3 mile to the point where an old roadbed joins from the right. Take this old roadbed to the second prominent side trail on the left, about 0.1 mile down the road. The first side trail you will pass runs a short distance out to the edge of a dangerous cliff overlooking the Cedar Creek gorge well above thundering Blue Hole Falls.

Follow the second side trail downhill to the creek just below **Cedar Falls**, a river wide 10-foot cascade. Cross the creek here and work your way downstream along the edge of the falls; *locate a safe place to cross*. This should not be too difficult under normal to low water conditions, but DO NOT attempt to cross if the water level is high.

Once across, work your way downstream along a steep, slippery path that becomes treacherously narrow as it descends along cascading Blue Hole Falls. The cascade begins fairly wide but narrows into a powerful sluice that cuts through the dark bedrock before spilling into a massive dark green plunge pool. The path does widen a bit as you descend past the lower cascade, but you'll need steady nerves to negotiate this route. There are dangers involved, but if you aren't intimidated about crossing steams and descending narrow paths along the edges of steep drop-offs, Blue Hole Falls will reward you with a scene of incredible beauty.

Chauga Narrows

Stream: Chauga Narrows   USGS Quadrangle: Whetstone, SC
Rating: excellent   Landowner: Sumter National Forest
Type: cascade/sluice   Trail length: 0.5 mile (one way)
Height: 25 feet   Difficulty: moderate (not suitable for children)
Stream flow: large   Elevation: approx. 1,360 feet

Directions

From Walhalla proceed west on Hwy. 28 for approximately 7 miles. Turn left onto Whetstone Road (S-193). Proceed west for 3.8 miles to the Chauga River at Blackwell bridge. Cross the bridge and turn left into a small parking area alongside the river. The trail begins here.

cascade at the upper end of the Chauga Narrows

Description

A 200-foot long section of the Chauga River about a half mile downstream of Whetstone Road could perhaps best be described as a "horizontal waterfall." From the small parking area adjacent to the bridge follow the old roadbed downstream for about 0.25 mile until it becomes a narrow path. Continue through a fairly substantial rhododendron thicket and proceed another 0.2 mile. As you near a right hand bend in the river you will begin to hear the roaring of falling water downstream. The path climbs slightly along the narrow riverbank and requires some caution to negotiate. As the path heads downstream well above the cascade look for a side path that drops down to the river around the middle of the Narrows. Another path is found just downstream that descends to the river near the base of the run.

This dramatic portion of the upper Chauga River begins with a steep 10-foot cascade then funnels into a rushing flume of water that drops about 20 feet over the next 50 yards. The water has cut a deep channel into the bedrock which is interrupted only by a narrow pillar of rock which divides the river at the base of the run. Use caution as you work your way along the west bank of the river. The rocks are extremely slippery and a swim here would be very unfortunate - perhaps fatal. If you're timing is just right and you visit when boaters are running this dynamo you are in for a real treat.

upper portion of the Chauga Narrows

Pigpen Falls

Stream: Licklog Creek

USGS Quadrangle: Satolah, Tamassee, SC, GA

Rating: excellent

Landowner: Sumter National Forest

Type: cascade

Trail length: 0.7 mile (one way)

Height: 25 feet

Difficulty: moderate

Stream flow: small

Elevation: approx. 1,760 feet

Directions

From Walhalla proceed west on Hwy. 28 for approximately 8.5 miles, then bear right onto SC 107. Proceed 3.2 miles and turn left onto Village Creek Road. Follow Village Creek Road for 1.8 miles then turn right onto Nicholson Ford Road (FS 775). Proceed 2.2 miles and park in the small parking area at the end of the road. If this lot is full turn around and drive about a half mile back to an alternate parking area just off Nicholson Ford Road.

Trail and description

The Bartram, Foothills, and Chattooga River Trials bisect this region and offer some of the best hiking around, and this short section is certainly no exception. The renowned Foothills Trail enters the woods at the northwest corner of the small parking area. Pass a fishermen's information box and continue down a gentle grade for 0.6 mile to a junction with the Chattooga River Trail. You'll come alongside splashing Licklog Creek shortly before reaching the trail junction. From here walk down a short hill to the edge of a large plunge pool facing the lower series of Pigpen's two splashing cascades. This pool is a favorite wading spot in the hot summer months.

Pigpen Falls

Licklog Falls

Stream: Licklog Creek
Rating: excellent
Type: cascade
Height: 25 feet, 40 feet
Stream flow: small

USGS Quadrangle: Satolah, Tamassee, SC, GA
Landowner: Sumter National Forest
Trail length: 0.8 mile (one way)
Difficulty: moderate to difficult
Elevation: approx. 1,720 feet

Directions
Follow the directions to Pigpen Falls.

Trail and description
        After passing Pigpen Falls cross a small wooden footbridge and
continue south on the Chattooga River Trail. In several hundred yards the trail
will pass enticingly close to the brink of the Licklog Falls' upper cascade. This
beautiful 25-foot waterslide rushes nearly vertically into a slender plunge pool.
A dangerously steep side path descends from the Chattooga River Trail toward
the base, but I consider it too dangerous to attempt. This route requires holding
onto roots and limbs as you descend and I won't recommend it. Best to enjoy
this one from the main trail, imperfect as the view is from that point.

*Lower Licklog Falls
tumbles into the
Chattooga River*

        Follow the Chattooga River Trail a bit further to the point where
another side trail, this one more prominent, angles to the right toward the
sound of yet more rushing water below. Descend along this much easier trail
down to the point where Licklog Creek rushes over a less spectacular series of
cascades just a few yards from the beautiful Chattooga River. The lower drop
totals perhaps 40 feet, though most of the drop is hidden by the thick streamside
underbrush. If you don't mind bushwhacking you can work your way back
upstream to the base of upper Licklog Falls, but it requires some effort and
presents the usual set of hazards such as slippery streamside rocks. From
whatever vantage point you choose these two waterfalls are quite scenic.

Big Bend Falls

Stream: Chattooga River USGS Quadrangle: Tamassee, SC, GA
Rating: excellent Landowner: Sumter National Forest
Type: cascade Trail length: 3.5 miles (one way)
Height: 30 feet total Difficulty: moderate
Stream flow: large Elevation: approx. 1,940 feet

Directions

From Walhalla proceed west on Hwy. 28 for approximately 8.5 miles, then bear right onto Hwy. 107. Proceed 10.4 miles and turn left onto Burrells Ford Road (FS 708). Drive 2.4 miles to the Burrells Ford Campground parking area on the left. The trail begins in the upper (southern) end of the parking area near the hiker's information board.

Description

Big Bend Falls is one of the largest single drops on the entire Chattooga River. This waterfall attracts relatively few visitors due to its isolated location and the distance from the closest (easily accessible) trailhead. The most popular route is the 7 mile round-trip hike from Burrells Ford. It's long, but by anyone's standard this is a magnificent walk.

This portion of the Chattooga River Trail features more beauty than can be practically described on these pages. Of special interest are the several segments of the trail that are nearly forced *into* the riverbed by the steep riverside terrain. There are dozens of magnificent vistas along the trail - take your time and enjoy the hike.

Trail description

Follow the Chattooga River Trail south from the campground parking lot. King Creek Falls is less than a mile from the trailhead and is only a short (15 minute) detour. At around the one mile point the trail intersects a riverside path which runs back upstream into Burrells Ford Campground. At mile 2.6 hikers must traverse several hundred feet of trail right alongside the river that could become impassable if the river is running high. Note: when the river is high, access Big Bend Falls via the Big Bend Trail.

The Big Bend Trail junction is at mile 2.9. (This alternate path winds 2.7 miles east out to Hwy. 107 and Cherry Hill Campground, offering an alternate trailhead if you have 2 vehicles.) Approximately 0.7 mile beyond this junction (3.5 miles from Burrells Ford) look for the side path about 20 yards from the base of a descending switchback. This path descends steeply through thick undergrowth toward the unmistakable roar of Big Bend Falls. Use caution viewing the falls as the riverside rocks are extremely slick.

King Creek Falls ★

Stream: King Creek
Rating: excellent
Type: cascade
Height: 70 feet total
Stream flow: medium

USGS Quadrangle: Tamassee, SC, GA
Landowner: Sumter National Forest
Trail length: 0.6 mile (one way)
Difficulty: moderate
Elevation: 2,200 feet

Directions

From Walhalla, proceed west on Hwy. 28 for approximately 8.5 miles, then bear right onto Hwy. 107. Proceed 10.4 miles and turn left onto Burrells Ford Road (FS 708). Drive 2.4 miles to the Burrells Ford campground parking area on the left. The trail begins in the upper (southern) end of the parking area near the visitor information board.

King Creek Falls

Trail and description

King Creek Falls is a surprisingly large cascade that requires a short 15 minute walk from the Burrells Ford campground parking area. Most of the walk to the waterfall is along the Chattooga River Trail. It traverses a pretty section of open woods before crossing splashing King Creek at mile 0.4. Cross the creek then turn left and follow the path upstream to the King Creek Falls spur trail. From here proceed up a moderate uphill grade for 0.2 mile to the base of this delightful cascade.

King Creek Falls plunges over a steep series of sloping ledges into a narrow log-choked ravine. A tiny plunge pool at the base stills the creek momentarily. This pool attracts waders in the summer months who are refreshed by King Creek's icy waters. Below the falls the creek begins cascading again as it completes its journey to the Chattooga River. Definitely do not miss this waterfall if you are in the area.

Spoonauger Falls

Stream: Spoonauger Creek
Rating: excellent
Type: cascade
Height: 60 feet total
Stream flow: small

USGS Quadrangle: Tamassee, SC, GA
Landowner: Sumter National Forest
Trail length: 0.5 mile (one way)
Difficulty: easy to moderate
Elevation: approx. 2,160 feet

Directions

From Walhalla proceed west on Hwy. 28 for approximately 8.5 miles, then bear right onto Hwy. 107. Proceed 10.4 miles and turn left onto Burrells Ford Road (FS 708). Drive approximately 3 miles to the Burrells Ford bridge. Park along the side of the road. Look for the Chattooga River Trail entering the woods on the north (upstream) side of the road about 100 yards before the bridge.

Spoonauger Falls

Trail and description

Like its nearby cousin to the south, Spoonauger Falls is a visitor-friendly cascade about a ten minute walk north of busy Burrells Ford. This splashing 60-foot cascade tumbles down a steep, striated cliff face into a narrow cove filled with rhododendron and shady hardwoods. From Burrells Ford Road take the Chattooga River Trail north into the river's floodplain and immediately enter the 9,000+ acre Ellicott Rock Wilderness. After approximately 0.3 mile of sidewalk-flat walking, rock hop across splashing Spoonauger Creek. Immediately after crossing the creek take the Spoonauger Falls spur trail to the right and walk up a series of steep switchbacks for 200 yards to the base of the pretty waterfall.

Station Cove Falls ★

Stream: Station Creek
Rating: excellent
Type: cascade
Height: 60 feet total
Stream flow: small

USGS Quadrangle: Walhalla, SC
Landowner: Sumter National Forest
Trail length: 0.7 mile (one way)
Difficulty: easy
Elevation: approx. 1,200 feet

Directions

From Walhalla proceed north on Hwy. 183. Turn left onto SC 11 (Cherokee Foothills Scenic Highway) and drive for 2 miles. Turn left onto Oconee Station Road (S-95). Drive 2.4 miles (0.3 mile past Oconee Station Historic Site) and park in the small gravel lot on the left.

Oconee Station Falls

Trail and description

Spilling delicately over a broken rock face, Station Cove Falls is located at the end of an easy, scenic 0.7 mile trail. Named for the nearby 18th century trading post, this peaceful cascade is quite impressive when the creek is up and conversely is reduced to a trickle during prolonged dry spells.

The trail to the cascade passes through a scenic open hardwood forest and skirts the edge of an old beaver pond that has largely filled in over the years and become marshland. An enormous shelf of flat rock extends from the base of the falls downstream, providing a great vantage point for photography or just finding a perfect spot to sit and enjoy the cascade. While you're in the area it's worth visiting Oconee Station to view the old wood and stone structure which served for a period as a fort on this portion of the Cherokee "frontier."

Lee Falls

Stream: Tamassee Creek
Rating: excellent
Type: cascade
Height: 75 feet
Stream flow: small

USGS Quadrangle: Tamassee, SC
Landowner: Sumter National Forest
Trail length: 1.5 miles (one way)
Difficulty: difficult
Elevation: approx. 1,500 feet

Directions

From Walhalla proceed north on SC 183. Turn left onto SC 11 (Cherokee Foothills Scenic Highway) and drive 4.5 miles. Turn left onto Cheohee Valley Road (S-172). Proceed 2.3 miles and turn onto Tamassee Knob Road (SR-95) on the left. Drive 0.5 mile to Jumping Branch Road on the right. Proceed along Jumping Branch Road for 1.4 miles to FS 715A on the left. Drive 0.6 mile to a parking area on the right just before the bridge.

Description

Rugged, isolated, difficult to reach, and quite beautiful - these are a few of the descriptions that can be applied to Lee Falls (aka Tamassee Falls) one of Oconee County's little-known waterfall gems. Interestingly, there is no official trail to the falls, and reaching it presents several challenges. If you possess a good overall sense of direction and a bit of determination you'll get there. Take your time and enjoy the walk.

From the parking area walk west along an old roadbed through a series of wildlife clearings. You actually have to ford the wide shallow creek twice in the first half of the hike, so be prepared to get your feet wet. The old road enters the hardwood forest at about mile 0.7. Follow the trail for approximately 0.25 mile and take a fork off to the left which crosses a small creek and heads in the direction of the larger branch of Tamassee Creek. Continue another 0.2 mile until it reaches Tamassee Creek then turn and follow it upstream until the trail becomes quite rocky and difficult to negotiate.

The final quarter mile is fairly rough, and warm-weather undergrowth further complicates the hike. The path crosses onto the south creek bank, passing the remains of an old rock smelter before approaching the base of the falls. Use a great deal of caution as the steep slopes around the base are littered with loose rocks. Those who persevere are rewarded with an incredibly wild scene as Tamassee Creek plunges vertically over a fragmented 75-foot cliff. The creek splits into at least three distinct tongues as it plunges into the isolated cove.

Lee Falls also known as Tamassee Falls

Lower Whitewater Falls ★

Stream: Whitewater River
Rating: spectacular
Type: cascade
Height: 200 feet
Stream flow: large

USGS Quadrangle: Reid, NC, SC
Landowner: Sumter National Forest
Trail length: 2 miles (one way)
Difficulty: moderate
Elevation: 1,800 feet

Directions

From Walhalla proceed north on SC 183. Turn left onto SC 11 (Cherokee Foothills Scenic Highway) and drive 14 miles. Turn left onto SC 130 and proceed 10.5 miles to the Duke Power Bad Creek Hydro Station on the right. Enter through an automatic gate (which only functions during daylight hours) and drive 2 miles to the Foothills Trail/Whitewater River parking area.

Description

Arguably as beautiful as its massive cousin several miles upstream, Lower Whitewater Falls is a must-see for every serious waterfall watcher. It's one of those rare escarpment waterfalls that overwhelms the senses. The main drop below the overlook is approximately 200 feet high, but this portion of the river drops an astounding 600 feet in about a quarter-mile as it plunges off the Blue Ridge escarpment shortly before merging with the beautiful waters of Lake Jocassee.

From the trailhead parking area follow the convenient blue blazes of the Lower Whitewater Falls spur trail. About 0.6 mile from the parking lot the trail crosses the raging Whitewater River well downstream of massive 400-foot Whitewater Falls. After crossing the bridge turn right and follow the Jocassee Gorges segment of the Foothills Trail northeast for 0.4 mile to the spur trail that winds 0.9 mile down to an observation deck that provides a bird's-eye view of the impressive cascade from several hundred yards away. There is currently no safe or practical way to approach the base of the cascade so simply enjoy this magnificent view from afar.

Whitewater Falls

Though it is located across the state line in North Carolina, Whitewater Falls is tantalizingly close - it's just a few minutes drive from the Lower Whitewater Falls parking area. And even better, the walk to see the falls is delightfully short. If Lower Whitewater Falls is on your list, go ahead and view its larger cousin while you are here. See page 131 for details.

South Carolina Hub #3
Pickens and Greenville Counties

    This expansive hub utilizes several of the most scenic highways in South Carolina and visits five of the upstate's most beautiful state parks. The waterfalls range from tiny intricate cascades to some of the most massive cataracts in this book. Waterfall watchers will be amazed at the beauty and power of the waterfalls in this region.

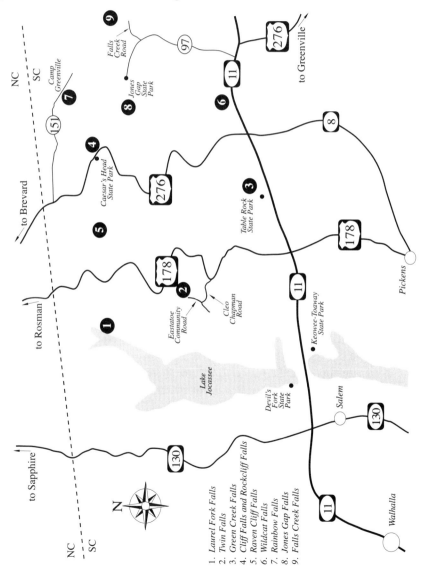

1. Laurel Fork Falls
2. Twin Falls
3. Green Creek Falls
4. Cliff Falls and Rockcliff Falls
5. Raven Cliff Falls
6. Wildcat Falls
7. Rainbow Falls
8. Jones Gap Falls
9. Falls Creek Falls

Laurel Fork Falls

Stream: Laurel Fork Creek
Rating: excellent
Type: cascade
Height: 80 feet
Stream flow: medium

USGS Quadrangle: Reid, NC, SC
Landowner: Sumter National Forest
Trail length: 20 minutes by boat
  on foot: 8.1 miles (one way)
Difficulty: difficult
Elevation: approx. 1,150 feet

Directions

By boat: from Walhalla drive northeast on SC 11 for approximately 15 miles. Turn left onto Jocassee Lake Road (S-25) and proceed to Devil's Fork State Park. Get an official lake map and follow the Toxaway River channel and turn east into the Laurel Fork finger of the lake.

On foot: this requires a strenuous 8.1 mile (one way) hike from the Laurel Valley Access point. From Pickens drive north on US 178 for approximately 16.5 miles. Turn left onto Laurel Valley Road (S-237). Turn onto the gravel road to the right and proceed 0.5 mile to the Laurel Valley Access parking area on the left. Because of the length of this trail hikers should obtain a Foothills Trail map or guidebook (www.foothillstrail.org).

Description

Magnificent Laurel Fork Falls tumbles directly into spectacular Lake Jocassee over a rugged 80-foot ledge. It's a tough 16 mile round trip via the shortest land route, realistically out of the reach of most visitors. It does make an ideal overnight destination for backpackers. However, if you have a small boat or don't mind hiring one of the local guides, viewing this gorgeous cascade is just a scenic boat ride away.

As you approach the waterfall by boat there is a fairly good view of the upper portions of the drop. However as you get closer much of the cascade is hidden from view behind a rocky buttress. It's possible to squeeze a small boat through the rocks into a tiny cove at the base of the falls that offers one of the most unique views of any waterfall in this guidebook.

Authors note: If you think photographing waterfalls on dry land is tricky try doing it from a boat bobbing around just a few feet from the base of a powerful waterfall. Hopefully in upcoming editions I'll return to Laurel Fork Falls and come up with an image suitable for print.

Twin Falls ★

Stream: Reedy Cove Creek	USGS Quadrangle: Eastatoe Gap, SC, NC
Rating: excellent	Landowner: Eastatoe Community Park
Type: cascade/free-fall	Trail length: 0.25 mile (one way)
Height: 75 feet	Difficulty: easy
Stream flow: medium	Elevation: 1,200 feet

Directions

From Pickens drive north on U.S. 178 for approximately 12 miles
(3.3 miles north of SC 11). Turn left onto Cleo Chapman Road (look for
Bob's Place Tavern on the left). Proceed 2 miles down the winding road to the
intersection. Turn right onto Eastatoe Community Road (S-92) and drive one
mile to Waterfalls Road on the right. Turn here and proceed 0.4 mile to a small
dirt parking area at the end of the road.

Twin Falls

Description

Twin Falls goes by several different names including Eastatoe Falls,
Rock Falls and Reedy Cove Falls. Whatever name you decide upon, it is
simply a superb destination. Catch it at high water (see above photo) and you'll
be absolutely enthralled by its power and charm.

A delightfully short 0.25 mile roadbed leads up to a covered observation deck across from the open base of the double drop. The left tongue free-

falls about 75 feet over a sheer cliff, while the right tongue cascades over several steep ledges before sliding over the lower half of the drop. At higher water levels a third tongue develops even further to the right and is partially visible crashing down a rocky channel beneath the forest canopy.

Green Creek Falls

Stream: Green Creek
Rating: excellent
Type: cascade
Height: 25 feet
Stream flow: medium

USGS Quadrangle: Table Rock, SC, NC
Landowner: Table Rock State Park
Trail length: 0.4 mile (one way)
Difficulty: moderate
Elevation: approx. 1,250 feet

Directions

From Pickens drive north on U.S. 178 for approximately 9 miles to SC 11. Turn right and drive east for 4.3 miles to the east entrance for Table Rock State Park (note: there is a $2 per vehicle entrance fee). Continue to the large parking area by the lake. Cross the street and proceed to the trailhead at the interpretive center.

Trail and description

Follow the paved trail beyond the interpretive center and tiny Carrick Creek Falls. Walk 0.2 mile and fork right onto the Table Rock Trail and climb uphill 0.2 mile to the falls on the left. Follow a steep, slippery scramble path to the base; it may be easier to leave the main trail about 100 yards before you

actually get to the waterfall. Look for the trailblaze located on a tree about the time you actually hear the waterfall. Veer off to the left and walk through the relatively open woods up to the base. The terrain is a bit cluttered but stays level most of the way. The best view of the falls is from the opposite bank but crossing the creek and staying dry is tricky.

Green Creek Falls

The beautiful 25-foot falls on Green Creek is extremely photogenic. At normal water levels it features dozens of tiny horizontal ledges which create a beautiful stair-stepping effect. There are a few drawbacks here - there is a large downed tree at the base which obscures a portion of the falls and the side trail leading down is somewhat of an adventure, especially if the ground is wet. It's a fairly easy hike, a beautiful park, and a worthy destination - a pretty good combination.

Cliff Falls

Stream: Cliff Creek
Rating: good
Type: cascade
Height: 35 feet
Stream flow: small

USGS Quadrangle: Cleveland, SC
Landowner: Caesar's Head State Park
Trail length: 0.8 mile (one way)
Difficulty: moderate
Elevation: approx. 2,500 feet

Directions

Follow U.S. 276 north from SC 11 for 10 minutes to Caesars Head State Park. Park at the visitors center on the west side of the highway.

Trail and description

Locate the Frank Coggins Trail across the highway from the visitor center and follow the purple blazes for 0.5 mile to the intersection with the Coldspring Connector Trail. Continue on the Frank Coggins Trail for an additional 0.2 mile. The trail splits here - take the left fork. Continue another 0.1 mile to the Rim of the Gap Trail. Turn left onto the Rim of the Gap Trail and walk about 25 yards to a side trail on the left that drops to the base of the waterfall.

Pretty Cliff Falls is worth a visit if rainfall has been average to good. Cliff Creek is a fairly small stream and when the weather has been dry this cascade diminishes greatly. The walk requires a bit of climbing along the beautifully wooded trail. The side trail descending to the base of the waterfall can be quite tricky as there are few limbs or roots to hold onto. If the water level is at least normal, Cliff Creek enthusiastically tumbles over a steep broken ledge into a narrow cove littered with large boulders. As with all small branch waterfalls, if it's been dry you may not want to hike solely to view the waterfall.

If the creek level is up and Cliff Falls is flowing well, you may wish to continue and visit two more small cascades. The first is the colorfully named

Firewater Falls, which is actually little more than a heavy drizzle under normal conditions. Named for a moonshining enterprise once located near the falls, Firewater Falls virtually disappears when it has been dry for an extended time. To reach Firewater, continue past Cliff Falls and turn onto the Naturaland Trust Trail (pink blazes). It's about a quarter mile past Cliff Falls. To reach yet another cascade, Rockcliff Falls, continue along the Naturaland Trust Trail to a point where it crosses U.S. 276. Cross the highway, reenter the woods and continue 0.3 mile until you reach this small waterfall which tumbles over a moss and lichened-covered rock wall. Total distance from the parking area to Rockcliff Falls is approximately 1.6 miles. Obtain a copy of the park's trail system map to be sure you stay on the right course.

Raven Cliff Falls ★

Stream: Matthews Creek
Rating: spectacular
Type: cascades/free-fall
Height: 420 feet
Stream flow: large

USGS Quadrangle: Table Rock, SC, NC
Landowner: Mountain Bridge Wilderness
Trail length: 2.2 miles (one way)
Difficulty: moderately strenuous (elevation change)
Elevation: approx. 2,800 feet

Directions

Caesar's Head State Park is located on Hwy. 276, approximately 6 miles north of SC 11 and 3 miles south of the North Carolina line. To reach the Raven Cliffs Falls trailhead continue north beyond the park for 1.1 miles. Turn right into the Raven Cliffs Falls parking area. *Carefully* walk across U.S. 276 to the Raven Cliffs Falls Trail (red blazes). Note: visitor fee required.

Trail and description

Spectacular Raven Cliff Falls is sure to make everyone's top 10 list of southern Appalachian waterfalls. Comparable to North Carolina's Whitewater Falls, Raven Cliff Falls shares several attributes with its mighty cousin to the southwest. Both waterfalls occur on sizable streams, and both descend in multiple stages from the eastern flank of the rugged Blue Ridge escarpment. The escarpment, also known as the "Blue Wall," is evident as you drive along SC 11, the Cherokee Foothills Scenic Highway. A massive wall of peaks and ridges rises dramatically from the Foothills region, providing the necessary geology to create large waterfalls such as those on the Whitewater, Thompson and Horsepasture Rivers, as well as here along Matthews Creek.

Though Caesar's Head State Park is generally associated with the waterfall it actually is located in the Mountain Bridge Wilderness. From the parking area cross the highway and be sure to sign the trail registry (mandatory). Follow the red-blazed Raven Cliffs Trail (#11) downhill into the forest. Most of the elevation loss occurs over the first 0.25 mile and the last 0.75 mile as you near an observation platform. The first segment of the trail runs 1.5 miles to a junction with the Gum Gap Trail (#13) at a very nice trail shelter perfect for picnics. Turn left at this junction and continue an additional 0.7 mile to the observation platform overlooking Raven Cliff Falls.

An abundance of hiking opportunities can be found in this portion of the Mountain Bridge Wilderness. At the 1.4 mile point of the Raven Cliffs Trail, hikers can veer right onto the blue-blazed Gum Gap Trail and walk 1.5 miles to the Naturaland Trust Trail (#14). This trail proceeds 0.5 mile down to a dramatic wood and steel suspension bridge spanning Matthews Creek just upstream from the brink of Raven Cliff Falls. Another option for the truly insane is an 8.5 mile loop involving the Dismal Trail and the Naturaland Trail. This option subjects hikers to a steep 1,200 feet descent to the bottom of the gorge and back up. Whatever your choice of trails you should obtain a copy of the Mountain Bridge Wilderness trail guide produced by the Naturaland Trust. You can obtain a copy at the Caesar's Head State Park visitor center or at nearby Jones Gap State Park.

*an older view of the falls from
a decommissioned overlook*

Wildcat Falls

Stream: Wildcat Branch
Rating: good
Type: cascades
Height: 30 feet/100 feet
Stream flow: small

USGS Quadrangle: Cleveland, SC
Landowner: Mountain Bridge Wilderness
Trail length: 0.4 mile (one way)
Difficulty: moderate
Elevation: approx. 1,200 feet

Directions

From Greenville take U.S. 276 north to where it joins SC 11. Turn left and follow U.S. 276/SC 11 west for 4.9 miles to a large pull-off on the right. If you are coming from the west the pull-off is located one half mile east of the intersection where U.S. 276 splits off and heads north toward Caesar's Head State Park. The lower cascade is plainly visible from this pull-off and it is not uncommon for quite a few automobiles to be parked here.

lower falls on Wildcat Branch

Description

Wildcat Falls is one of those nice two-for-one destinations that offers two very different waterfall experiences. The first cascade is a pretty two-tiered drop just a stone's throw from the busy highway. An upper plunge of about 10 feet is immediately followed by a slanting 20 foot waterslide. An enormous plunge pool stills Wildcat Branch below the cascade and more than a few visitors wade and swim here in the hot summer months. The number of motorists who stop to view this small cascade is quite high and snack vendors are known to set up shop here in the summer and fall.

Wildcat's other attraction requires a bit more work to appreciate. A relatively easy 0.4 mile trail runs along the creek up to a much wilder waterfall. Follow the steps to the left of the pool and cross the creek via an old wooden footbridge. Follow the path for several hundred yards past the remains of an old homestead once reportedly used as a caretaker's home for the "wayside park" along the highway. All that remains today is an old stone fireplace and rock floor. Continue past the ruins and cross another footbridge. Follow the path upstream for about 0.3 mile to the "end of trail" sign at the base of a massive granite cliff. Here Wildcat Branch makes a sliding descent down the face of an open rock wall into a boulder-studded cove. You will have to do some minor climbing and maneuvering among the boulders to get a good view. If the creek is up, the waterfall is well worth the walk as it cascades and slides down the steep rock face.

Note: If Wildcat Branch is barely flowing at the footbridge there won't be much to see at the upper falls. Save your time and energy and visit another time.

Upper Wildcat Falls
at the end of the trail

Rainbow Falls

Stream: Cox Camp Creek
Rating: excellent
Type: free-fall
Height: 100 feet
Stream flow: medium

USGS Quad: Standingstone Mtn., NC, SC
Landowner: YMCA Camp Greenville
Trail length: 0.5 mile (one way)
Difficulty: strenuous (not for children)
Elevation: approx. 2,900 feet

Directions

From the junction of U.S. 276 and SC 11 follow U.S. 276 for approximately 6 miles to Caesar's Head State Park. Continue 2.5 miles past the park entrance to Solomon Jones Road on the right (look for the Camp Greenville sign). Proceed 4.5 miles to a small gravel parking area just past a crosswalk on the right.

Trail and description

From the parking pull-off walk back to the crosswalk sign and turn south. Descend steeply to Cox Camp Creek, then turn north (right) and begin climbing upstream. Carefully cross the creek using a wire cable strung across the creek just below a prominent set of cascades well below the main waterfall. View the falls from downstream from one of the large boulders. Use extreme care in this area as the rocks can be very slippery and creek crossings can be dangerous at any time.

This 100 foot beauty spills over a rugged cliff into a boulder-strewn ravine. The cliff is stained an unusual combination of dark grey and tan adding to the ambience of the location. Coincidentally the appearance of the waterfall is reminiscent of Rainbow Falls in the Great Smoky Mountains National Park. The trail descends *very steeply* to the falls (approximate 400 foot elevation change) and is definitely not for those who are in poor physical condition or are afraid of heights. Also, because the waterfall is on private property, be sure to obtain permission, follow all posted rules and regulations, and treat the property with extreme respect. Camp Greenville does not allow visitors to use the trail after heavy rainfall or under icy conditions. Camp Greenville's number is (864) 836-3291.

Note: The waterfall can also be accessed via a 5 mile round trip hike from Jones Gap State Park. This route approaches the waterfall from below. If you choose to hike in by this route and you arrive at the falls only to find a group from the camp, please be respectful that you are a guest on their property.

Jones Gap Falls

Stream: Middle Saluda tributary   USGS Quad: Cleveland, SC
Rating: excellent   Landowner: Jones Gap State Park
Type: cascade   Trail length: 1.3 miles (one way)
Height: 50 feet   Difficulty: moderate
Stream flow: medium   Elevation: approx. 1,400 feet

Directions

From Greenville take U.S. 276 north for approximately 25 miles to the junction with SC 11 in Cleveland. Follow U.S. 276 for an additional 1.4 miles and turn right onto River Falls Road (S-97). Proceed five miles to Jones Gap State Park. Turn right into the parking area. Follow a 0.3 mile path across the beautiful Middle Saluda River from the parking area upstream to the trailhead just beyond the park headquarters building.

Trail and description

The 1.3 (one way) hike to pretty 50-foot Jones Gap Falls follows the beautiful Middle Saluda River upstream through a magnificent wilderness setting. Begin your hike at the information board next to the automobile bridge that spans the beautiful stream. Registration forms are available for hikers to fill out before you begin.

Follow the delightful trail for about 0.6 mile to a fork, then veer left to stay on the Jones Gap Trail. The path seldom strays more than a stone's throw from the picturesque Middle Saluda. Continue another 0.6 mile to the John Reid Clonts Memorial footbridge. Cross the bridge, veer left and walk approximately 200 yards. Pass campsite 11 then cross a tributary stream via a series of stepping stones; turn right onto a short spur trail which leads up to the base of the waterfall.

Jones Gap Falls

Falls Creek Falls ★

Stream: Falls Creek   USGS Quad: Standingstone Mountain, NC, SC
Rating: excellent   Landowner: Mountain Bridge Wilderness
Type: cascade   Trail length: 1.4 miles (one way)
Height: 125 feet   Difficulty: strenuous/not for children
Stream flow: medium   Elevation: approx. 2,200 feet

Directions

From Greenville take U.S. 276 north for approximately 25 miles to the junction with SC 11 in Cleveland. Follow U.S. 276 for an additional 1.4 miles and turn right onto River Falls Road (S-97). Proceed 4 miles and turn right onto Duckworth Road. Drive 0.5 mile to Falls Creek Road on the right. Drive 0.4 mile (note Palmetto Bible Camp on the right), cross a small bridge and park on the left side of the road at the tiny pull-off. Register at the kiosk here.

Trail and description

If you're up for a good cardio workout the 1.4 mile trek to Falls Creek Falls is just your ticket. The hike to this underrated cascade gains nearly 1,000 vertical feet and is not for those unaccustomed to strenuous hikes. From the trailhead parking area follow orange blazes along an old roadbed uphill. The first 0.4 mile climbs moderately before leveling off, but if you struggle in this initial portion go ahead and turn around as it gets much tougher just ahead. The trail rock hops across Little Falls Creek at mile 0.7. The next 0.4 mile seems much longer as it steeply climbs up toward the waterfall, often within earshot of tumbling Falls Creek. There are a few traditional switchbacks but much of this portion of the trail is just plain steep and requires great effort.

Just beyond the 1.2 mile point the trail passes beneath a prominent rock outcropping just as it offers your first view of the cascade from several hundred yards away. This view is outstanding in the leafless winter months and provides a great overview of the impressive size of this waterfall. The trail drops down along the scenic midpoint of the waterfall before descending past the lower cascades. Visit Falls Creek Falls at high water and the scene is spectacular. At lower levels it does not possess the "wow" factor but is still a very worthy cascade. The photo on the next page was taken the day after a 3" rain - the spray was so thick that I could not keep the lens dry for a good shot. The trail crosses the creek at the base of the falls utilizing ropes and chains and continues beyond the waterfall, eventually connecting with the Hospital Rock Trail that runs to Jones Gap State Park. Total hiking distance if you choose this combination of trails is about 7 miles.

*Late autumn at
a rain swollen
Falls Creek Falls*

Section III

southwestern
North Carolina

North Carolina Hub #1 - Highlands & Franklin

The North Carolina mountains offer some of the most outstanding waterfalls anywhere in the entire Appalachian chain, and there are few falls as impressive, or as easy to view, as those found near the beautiful town of Highlands. This popular resort town is known for its upscale homes and prestigious country clubs and touts itself as one of the highest incorporated towns east of the Mississippi. Sitting at a lofty elevation of over 4,000 feet atop the rugged Highlands plateau, this area certainly possesses the topography for big waterfalls. Factor in abundant rainfall (the area has one of the highest annual rainfall averages in the continental United States) of over 80 inches per year and you'll find that Highlands and Franklin offer up plenty of waterfall action.

Follow spectacular U.S. 64 west down the rugged Cullasaja gorge to bustling Franklin then continue southwest on to yet two more highly scenic cascades along short trails deep within the remote Standing Indian Wilderness.

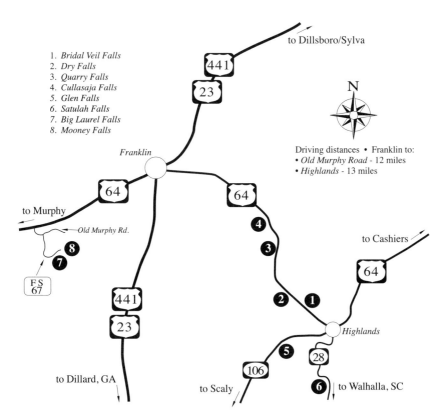

1. Bridal Veil Falls
2. Dry Falls
3. Quarry Falls
4. Cullasaja Falls
5. Glen Falls
6. Satulah Falls
7. Big Laurel Falls
8. Mooney Falls

to Dillsboro/Sylva

N

Driving distances • Franklin to:
• Old Murphy Road - 12 miles
• Highlands - 13 miles

Franklin

to Murphy

Old Murphy Rd.

to Cashiers

to Dillard, GA

to Scaly

to Walhalla, SC

Highlands

Falls of the Cullasaja Gorge

The seven mile drive from Lake Sequoyah dam to the bottom of the Cullasaja Gorge is a near continuous run of falling water. Through this rugged gorge the mighty Cullasaja plunges over 1,400 feet into a beautiful valley just east of Franklin then merges with the historic Little Tennessee River. Two major waterfalls, two other lesser falls and dozens of various shoals and cascades are sprinkled throughout this magnificent stretch. Scenic U.S. 64 is seldom more than a stone's throw away, providing great access to this splendid ribbon of cascading water. There are dozens of pull-offs which allow visitors to view the scenery or scramble down the banks to see the sights up close.

Bridal Veil Falls

Stream: Bridal Veil Creek	USGS Quad: Highlands, NC, GA
Rating: good	Landowner: Nantahala National Forest
Type: cascade/free-fall	Trail length: roadside
Height: 60 feet	Difficulty: n/a
Stream flow: small	Elevation: 3,560 feet

Directions

From the intersection of U.S. 64 and Hwy. 106 in Highlands drive west on U.S. 64 for 2.3 miles. The pull-off for the waterfall is on the right side of the road. If you are remotely awake you won't have any trouble finding it.

Description

Bridal Veil is one of the area's best known waterfalls, but not because the waterfall itself is overly impressive. Bridal Veil has been an attraction since the original highway was constructed in the late 1920s when it actually ran *behind* the waterfall. Following a series of upper cascades tiny Bridal Veil Creek launches into the air for a 40-foot plunge beside the highway. Even after

traffic rumbles by Bridal Veil Falls; access behind the falls is blocked due to falling ice.

modernization of the highway in 1959 which bypassed this unique experience, motorists could still pull off the main road and drive behind the waterfall. Access behind the falls was closed in the early 2000s when a huge chunk of the cliff wall broke off and blocked the road behind the falls. It has been cleared in recent years and once again you can enjoy this unusual motoring experience.

Below the waterfall the stream flows beneath the highway before spilling into the Cullasaja River. Keep in mind that despite its reputation, Bridal Veil Falls can be disappointing when it's dry. Catch it during an extreme winter and the cliff face can become a nearly solid column of ice.

Dry Falls ★

Stream: Cullasaja River
Rating: spectacular
Type: cascade/free-fall
Height: 70 feet
Stream flow: large

USGS Quad: Highlands, NC, GA
Landowner: Nantahala National Forest
Trail length: 200
Difficulty: easy; some steps involved
Elevation: 3,320 feet

*midwinter at
Dry Falls*

Directions

From the intersection of U.S. 64 and Hwy. 106 in Highlands drive west on U.S. 64 for 3.1 miles. The parking area is located on the left side of the road - use caution turning into the parking area as the visibility along this portion of the highway isn't that great. There is a donation box located here encouraging support of efforts to improve the facilities.

Description

Don't let the name fool you - Dry Falls can be quite a wet experience. A paved footpath drops from a newly constructed parking area providing a beautiful view of this free-falling veil of exploding water. Continue along the path and you'll soon find yourself behind the thundering veil as the path traverses a deep recess in the cliff. The noise is deafening behind the cascade. The path continues to the far side of the river to an observation point around the midpoint of the cascade. This spot allows a better view of the lower cascades.

Dry Falls is one of the most popular waterfalls in the region due to its proximity to town and its short, easy trail. If you come on the weekends or at the height of tourist season you may have to wait for a parking place. The waterfall is absolutely delightful early in the morning when you may have it all to yourself. For those who can't handle steps, an elongated deck stretching from the parking area allows a nice view of Dry Falls from above.

Quarry Falls

Stream: Cullasaja River
Rating: excellent
Type: cascade
Height: 20 feet
Stream flow: large

USGS Quad: Scaly Mountain, NC
Landowner: Nantahala National Forest
Trail length: roadside
Hazards: slippery rocks, fast current
Elevation: 2,840 feet

Directions

From the intersection of U.S. 64 and Hwy. 106 in Highlands, drive west on U.S. 64 for 6.4 miles. There is a pull-off here that offers an excellent view of this multi-tiered drop.

Quarry Falls

Description

Quarry Falls is really known more as a recreational destination than a waterfall, but it is very scenic in its own right. Also known as "bust-your-butt" falls, this easily viewed waterfall is formed as the Cullasaja is constricted and races over a series of three ledges. In the warm summer months it is overrun with throngs of people who jump, swim and slide in the dangerous waters. It is unfortunately the scene of all too many accidents. As if the fast falling water was not enough, the steep smooth banks alongside the cascade are treacherously slippery and injuries due to slips and falls are common. The name came from the area just across the highway which was quarried decades ago for the rock necessary for the construction of U.S. 64.

Cullasaja Falls ★

Stream: Cullasaja River	USGS Quad: Scaly Mountain, NC
Rating: spectacular	Landowner: Nantahala National Forest
Type: cascade/free-fall	Trail length: roadside
Height: 200+ feet	Hazards: heavy traffic, steep drop-offs
Stream flow: large	Elevation: 2,840 feet

Directions

From the intersection of U.S. 64 and Hwy. 106 in Highlands drive west on U.S. 64 for 8.7 miles. There are several very small, narrow pull-offs on the left (opposite) side of the road. Because of the dangerous curves along this section of the highway and the distracted nature of many drivers trying to view the waterfall, drivers are encouraged to continue down the road for a mile or so, turn around, then come back and pull off to the right.

Description

Cullasaja Falls is the undisputed king of the Cullasaja's waterfalls, and is in fact one of the most impressive waterfalls in the Southern Appalachian region. At normal to high water levels it is absolutely spectacular. Conversely, during prolonged dry spells there is more cliff than waterfall and Cullasaja Falls becomes little more than a pretty curiosity. Catch it when the river is up and you may even have trouble viewing the cascade due to the incredible amount of mist and spray wafting up from the base.

While it is possible to scramble to the base for a look, the view is really not any better. It's a steep descent and only the lower portions of the cascade are visible from the base, so save you strength (and your neck) and enjoy the majesty of Cullasaja Falls from the (relative) safety of the "viewing area" along the highway. By the way, you may have noticed that the route for U.S. 64 was literally blasted into the sheer cliffs above the gorge here at Cullasaja Falls. There are more than a few motorists who simply will not travel from Franklin to Highlands via U.S. 64.

Kevin Adams, in his wonderful work *North Carolina Waterfalls* calls this location this most dangerous traffic situation in the mountains due to the treacherous combination of "narrow road, blind curves, sheer drop-offs, and waterfall gawkers..." Well said - be very careful here. I have personally witnessed people leaving their parked cars partially in the highway; others attempt to take photographs while standing in oncoming traffic. As someone once said, "you can't fix stupid."

Cullasaja Falls

Glen Falls ★

Stream: East Fork Overflow Creek
Rating: excellent
Type: cascade/free-fall
Height: 20 - 70 feet
Stream flow: small

USGS Quad: Highlands, NC, GA
Landowner: Nantahala National Forest
Trail length: 1 mile (one way)
Hazards: strenuous
Elevation: 3,400 feet

Directions

From the intersection of U.S. 64 and Hwy. 106 in Highlands drive south on Hwy. 106 for 1.7 miles. Turn left at the Glen Falls sign, then take an immediate right onto #1618. Proceed 1 mile to the trailhead parking area.

Trail and description

The hike to view all of the large cascades that comprise Glen Falls is what is sometimes known as a "lung buster." This nearly 1 mile (one way) path drops around 700 vertical feet alongside the plunging East Fork of Overflow Creek, a major Chattooga River tributary. It's difficult to actually assign a height to these cascades as it is a near continuous chain of falling water. Several stand out and are quite worthy in their own right. This popular trail features three major drops ranging from about 20 feet high to nearly 70 feet. Short spur paths branch off the main trail and provide access to some of the more scenic minor drops as well. Roughly speaking, it is approximately 0.4 mile to the base of the first falls, another 0.3 mile to the base of the second, and about another 0.2 mile to a smaller, third falls.

Outstanding vistas of Blue Valley can be glimpsed just below the trailhead. The hike is a great workout, but you'll only enjoy the entire trek if you're in good physical condition. Due to its proximity to Highlands the trail can become quite congested during the tourist season, particularly on the weekends - plan your trip accordingly. Also keep in mind that these waterfalls are quite sensitive to dry conditions.

Glen Falls

Lower Satulah Falls

Stream: Clear Creek
Rating: good
Type: cascading waterslide
Height: over 100 feet
Stream flow: small

USGS Quad: Highlands, NC, GA
Landowner: Nantahala National Forest
Trail length: roadside
Hazards: n/a
Elevation: 3,000 feet

Directions

From the intersection of U.S. 64 and Hwy. 28 in downtown Highlands, take Hwy. 28 south for 3.6 miles and park in the pull-off on the right.

Description

Lower Satulah Falls also goes by the name Clear Creek Falls or Hidden Falls. This steep waterslide is easily visible from the roadside overlook as it emerges ever so briefly from the dense canopy of the Nantahala National Forest. The waterfall is pretty, but the overall view here is even more impressive as scenic Blue Valley unfolds before you. The massive profile of Georgia's second highest peak, Rabun Bald, rises majestically to the south. Lower Satulah Falls is easier to see in the leafless winter months, and during the summer and fall its flow can be greatly diminished.

Logic dictates that if there is a Lower Satulah Falls, there must be an Upper Satulah Falls as well. Indeed there is but it is located on private property. If you head back towards Highlands proceed about 1.25 miles and you'll pass this pretty waterslide as you drive along the rugged southern slopes of majestic Satulah Mountain.

Big Laurel Falls ★

Stream: Big Laurel Branch
Rating: excellent
Type: cascade
Height: 25 feet
Stream flow: small

USGS Quad: Rainbow Springs, NC
Landowner: Nantahala National Forest
Trail length: 0.6 mile (one way)
Difficulty: easy to moderate
Elevation: 3,880 feet

Directions

From the intersection of U.S. 441 and U.S. 64 in Franklin proceed west on U.S. 64 for 11.8 miles and turn left onto Old Murphy Road (note the sign for Standing Indian Campground). Drive 1.9 miles to Wallace Gap, then turn right onto FS 67. Proceed 1.7 miles to a fork. Stay left (the right fork leads into the campground). The paved road becomes gravel at this point. You will pass a gate that is often closed in the winter months due to poor or icy road conditions. If it is closed do not attempt to reach the falls. If it is open proceed 5 miles to a small pull-off on the right. There is a sign here for the Laurel Falls Trail and Timber Ridge Trail.

Big Laurel Falls

Trail and description

Beyond the trail sign begin walking and immediately turn right. In about two hundred feet cross Mooney Creek over a footbridge and come to an intersection. Turn right and follow the Big Laurel Trail downstream. The path soon leaves Mooney Creek and bends left as it begins following Kilby Creek upstream past the point where Big Laurel Branch merges.

The fairly easy hike is a good one for children. The cascade is splendidly secluded in a lush cove and tumbles playfully over a series of rocky ledges framed by beautiful native rhododendron. A large plunge pool at the base of the cascade completes the near beautiful scene.

Mooney Falls

Stream: Mooney Creek
Rating: good
Type: cascade
Height: 15 feet (lower cascade)
Stream flow: small

USGS Quad: Prentiss, NC
Landowner: Nantahala National Forest
Trail length: 200 yards (one way)
Difficulty: easy
Elevation: 4,000 feet

Directions

From the intersection of U.S. 441 and U.S. 64 in Franklin proceed west on U.S. 64 for 11.8 miles and turn left onto Old Murphy Road (note the sign for Standing Indian Campground). Drive 1.9 miles to Wallace Gap, then turn right onto FS 67. Proceed 1.7 miles to a fork. Stay left (the right fork leads into the campground). The paved road becomes gravel at this point. You will pass a gate here that is usually closed in the winter months due to poor or icy road conditions. If it is closed you cannot drive to the falls. If it is open proceed 5.2 miles to the pull-off marked by the Mooney Falls sign on the right.

Description

A short 200 yard path descends to a scenic series of cascades known as Mooney Falls. A lesser known name is Hemp Patch Branch Falls. One leg of the path accesses a nice vantage point at the top of the main drop; the other winds down to the base. Though none of the cascades is particularly large, the cumulative effect is quite nice. The series culminates in a steep 15-foot cascade that can be easily enjoyed from the streambank though the cascade is often littered with limbs, logs and other forest debris. This is one of those waterfalls that I actually like better each time I visit.

*Mooney Falls
lower cascade*

North Carolina Hub #2 - Cashiers & Sapphire

All of the North Carolina hubs feature excellent waterfalls and the falls in the vicinity of Cashiers and Sapphire are no exception. In fact, some of the most dramatic waterfalls in the eastern U. S. are located here. Other falls range from minor cascades to some of the largest in the region. One of the absolute must-see falls is Whitewater Falls, one of the highest major waterfalls in the east. Other major waterfalls occur in the Thompson, Horsepasture and Toxaway gorges as these rivers transition from the lofty escarpment region

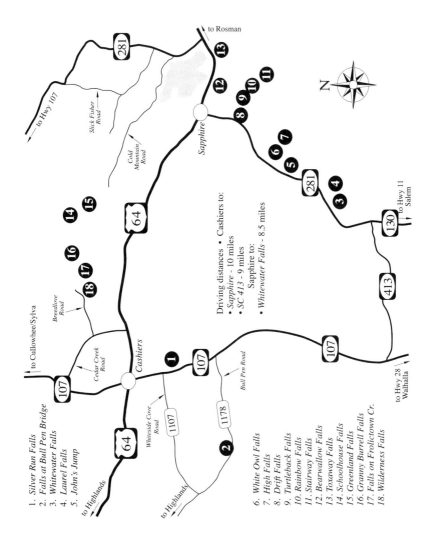

Driving distances • Cashiers to:
• Sapphire - 10 miles
• SC 413 - 9 miles
Sapphire to:
• Whitewater Falls - 8.5 miles

1. Silver Run Falls
2. Falls at Bull Pen Bridge
3. Whitewater Falls
4. Laurel Falls
5. John's Jump
6. White Owl Falls
7. High Falls
8. Drift Falls
9. Turtleback Falls
10. Rainbow Falls
11. Stairway Falls
12. Bearwallow Falls
13. Toxaway Falls
14. Schoolhouse Falls
15. Greenland Falls
16. Granny Burrell Falls
17. Falls on Frolictown Cr.
18. Wilderness Falls

to the Foothills region of the South Carolina piedmont. Amazingly, only a small portion of the waterfalls in this region are shown here. There are literally dozens of other great cascades to visit, but I have tried to include only those that are relatively easy to find and visit. A guidebook such as Kevin Adams' excellent compilation *North Carolina Waterfalls* can take you to all the great falls that the tarheel state state has to offer.

Once you visit all this area has to offer in the way of falling water, be sure to visit the bustling town of Cashiers. Once a quiet crossroads hamlet, the town has virtually exploded into a coveted vacation and second home mecca known for its incredible natural beauty. The Cashiers valley is virtually surrounded by magnificent peaks featuring exposed rock walls and cliffs.

Silver Run Falls ★

Stream: Silver Run Creek
Rating: excellent
Type: free-fall/waterslide
Height: 40 feet (total drop)
Stream flow: small

USGS Quad: Cashiers, NC, GA, SC
Landowner: Nantahala National Forest
Trail length: 200+ yards (one way)
Difficulty: easy
Elevation: 3,320 feet

Directions to the trailhead

From the intersection of U.S. 64 and Hwy. 107 in Cashiers take Hwy. 107 south for 4.1 miles to the gravel pull-off on the left side of the road.

Trail description

Without doubt Silver Run Falls is the most popular waterfall in the Cashiers vicinity. This beauty spills gracefully over an undercut ledge into a broad plunge pool at the end of a short easy path. At higher water levels you can actually hear Silver Run Falls from the roadside parking area. Follow the gentle path through the woods across the footbridge spanning the headwaters of the Whitewater River. In the years preceding the footbridge, thousands of visitors ventured across a large fallen log to span the stream. More than a few ended up in the drink. If you're feeling adventurous the log is still there. Beyond the crossing you'll scramble over a few rocks and find yourself alongside the edge of Silver Run Falls' beautiful emerald-green plunge pool.

Description

    The waterfall slides down a series of upper shoals before free-falling momentarily, then intersecting the near-vertical rock face for a quick slide into a gorgeous plunge pool. This is a mandatory photo spot and there are several vantage points to choose from.

    Another smaller less scenic cascade is just above Silver Run, but accessing it requires a short, steep root-grabbing climb up the cliff to the left of the falls. It's really not worth the dangers or the effort. If you can't be dissuaded, don't go beyond the cascade as you would be exiting public land and entering private property.

*Silver Run Falls
near Cashiers*

Chattooga River at Bull Pen Bridge

Stream: Chattooga River   USGS Quad: Highlands, NC, GA
Rating: good   Landowner: Nantahala National Forest
Type: cascade   Trail length: roadside
Height: 15 feet   Difficulty: n/a
Stream flow: medium   Elevation: approx. 2,380 feet

Directions

    From the intersection of U.S. 64 and Hwy. 107 in Cashiers take Hwy. 107 south for about 6 miles. Turn right onto Bull Pen Road (#1178). Drive 5 miles to the one lane bridge spanning the river. Cross the bridge and park.

Description

    The old iron bridge in the area known locally as the Bull Pen spans the beautiful Chattooga River just above a highly scenic set of cascades. It's not much in the way of a vertical drop, but it is quite beautiful and doesn't require any effort to view (other than the bumpy ride). Powerful river currents have carved dozens of deep potholes (known as swirl holes) into the riverbed. The unusual combination of aerated water and huge boulders and rock slabs come together to create a magnificent wilderness scene.

    If you are looking for a great hike you can stretch your legs on the Chattooga Cliffs Trail which winds north from the bridge upriver for 5 miles to Whiteside Cove Road. This delightful trail gains about 300 feet in elevation but it feels like you're climbing even more. The trail spends a lot of time along the river but large portions snake back into the Chattooga watershed. The trail offers plenty of outstanding scenery including scenic shoals and beautiful pools.

cascades beneath
Bull Pen bridge

Whitewater Falls ★

Stream: Whitewater River
Rating: spectacular
Type: cascade/ free-fall
Height: 411 feet
Stream flow: large

USGS Quad: Cashiers, NC, GA, SC
Landowner: Nantahala National Forest
Trail length: 0.25 mile (one way) minimum
Difficulty: easy to moderate
Elevation: 2,560 feet

Directions

From the intersection of U.S. 64 and Hwy. 107 in Cashiers take Hwy. 107 south for 9.3 miles. Turn left onto SC 413 and proceed 2.2 miles to the stop sign. Turn left onto Hwy. 281 and proceed 1.2 miles to the Whitewater Falls Recreation Area on the right. From Sapphire at the U.S. 64/Hwy. 281 intersection follow Hwy. 281 south for 8.5 miles and turn left into Whitewater Falls. There is a nominal fee (currently $2 per vehicle) to park here.

*summer scene at
Whitewater Falls*

Description

Do not miss this spectacular waterfall. It's massive, majestic and one of the undisputed *great* falls in the region. Not only is Whitewater Falls an astounding 411 feet, but the Whitewater River is a stream of considerable volume. Here the lofty escarpment region dramatically plunges to the much lower foothills region of South Carolina creating many of the great falls that this region is known for. Whitewater Falls is such an impressive site that it has been designated for protection as a North Carolina Natural Heritage Area.

Over the last decade the parking area has received a dramatic and much needed facelift and new restrooms have been constructed. The Foothills Trail has also been rerouted to avoid congestion at the overlooks. This is one location where your visitors fees have obviously been put to good use.

The path to the upper overlook begins at the lower end of the parking area. It's slightly uphill, but still relatively easy. It's also paved and can accommodate persons in wheelchairs. The path stretches just a bit less than a quarter-mile to the upper overlook and provides a view from a vantage point roughly level with the brink of the falls, several hundred yards distant.

The view is nothing less than dramatic as Whitewater Falls booms over a massive cliff of fractured rock, descending in numerous tongues via dozens of cascades, free falls and water slides. If the water level is high the roar can be heard long before you see the waterfall. This is the most convenient spot to view Whitewater, but the *best* view can be found by following the steps just to the right of the upper overlook. Descend just over 150 steps to the lower overlook. Here the waterfall is framed beautifully by large hemlocks.

A short spur trail connects the lower overlook with the Foothills Trail, then continues a dramatic descent to the Whitewater River below the falls. Try to resist the urge to visit the base of the waterfall. It is a difficult bushwhack with no formal trail. It's also exceedingly dangerous due to the combination of slippery rocks and abundant spray from the carnage above. Perhaps even more

*heavy winter rains transform
Whitewater Falls into an amazing
spectacle of falling water*

important are the thriving populations of rare plants that live in the spray zone which could be harmed from visitors plowing through the area. This would be a bad place to suffer an injury. Best to enjoy the beauty of Whitewater Falls from the safety of the developed overlooks. *Note:* there have been hundreds of injuries and many deaths at Whitewater Falls over the years. Please observe all warning signs and stay away from the brink and base of the waterfall!

Don't forget: Lower Whitewater Falls isn't too far downstream. Because of its South Carolina location it has been included in the Oconee County, South Carolina section of the book. It's not quite as massive as Whitewater Falls, but it's awfully close. See page 102 for details.

Laurel Falls

Stream: Corbin Creek
Rating: good
Type: cascade/ free fall
Height: 400+ feet
Stream flow: small

USGS Quad: Cashiers, NC, SC, GA
Landowner: Nantahala National Forest
Trail length: 1.0 mile (one way)
Difficulty: strenuous; 400' change in elevation
Elevation: 2,560 feet

Directions to the trailhead
Follow the directions to Whitewater Falls.

Trail description
Walk to the upper Whitewater Falls overlook then descend just over 150 steps to the lower viewing deck. Take the short spur path that connects with the Foothills Trail. Turn left here and descend along a series of looping switchbacks to a steel footbridge that spans the rushing Whitewater River a short distance downstream from Whitewater Falls. Cross the bridge and follow the path downstream for several hundred yards to another footbridge spanning splashing Corbin Creek.

Description
Relatively few visitors view Laurel Falls as a destination waterfall. Though the relative height is about the same as Whitewater Falls the creek is small and much of it is hidden in dense streamside foliage. The lower 100 feet or so is quite scenic but is it worth the 400-foot vertical climb back out of the gorge? You'll have to decide for yourself but it does make for one heck of a workout.

John's Jump

Stream: Mill Creek
Rating: good
Type: cascade
Height: 25 feet
Stream flow: small

USGS Quad: Cashiers, NC, SC, GA
Landowner: Nantahala National Forest
Trail length: 100 yards (one way)
Difficulty: steep scramble
Elevation: 3,150 feet

Directions to the trailhead

From the intersection of U.S. 64 and Hwy. 281 in Sapphire take Hwy. 281 south for 4.85 miles. Park along the grassy shoulder on the left side of the highway and look for a steep overgrown path near the southern end of the highway guardrail.

Description

If you've never seen one, do your best to obtain a copy of Jim Bob Tinsley's fantastic book *The Land of Waterfalls* in which he documents the very best waterfalls in the Transylvania County area. In the book Tinsley provides a great deal of colorful history behind each waterfall. John's Jump reportedly got its name from Arthur Middleton "Chucky Joe" Huger who witnessed first hand a man named John Hinkle leap from a large rock to reach the bottom. Another local story claims that John died from his leap at the waterfall. Who really knows? But why change a good story?

This pretty cascade is just off the highway yet if you weren't looking for it you would drive right by. The cascade occurs on Mill Creek, a Thompson River tributary. The drop is fairly small and not particularly outstanding, but it's still a worthwhile stop as you motor along Hwy. 281 between Whitewater Falls and the waterfalls of the Horsepasture River. It requires a steep scramble to reach the base. Part of the path heads out to the brink of the falls but don't get too close - it's very slippery and not worth the risk; and we don't want to have to add another name to the legend of John's Jump.

Falls of the Thompson River Gorge

Not as well known as its neighbors to the immediate east and west, the Horsepasture and the Whitewater, there are several impressive waterfalls to be found on the Thompson River. The trouble is that there is not a good trail system leading to these waterfalls. Kevin Adams in *North Carolina Waterfalls* provides directions to 8 Thompson River waterfalls, and only one of them could really be classified as easy to reach - White Owl Falls. While I have been to several of these waterfalls, I have decided to only provide directions to the two that I consider fairly straight forward to access. If you are interested in exploring this magnificent area and its incredible collection of falling water, purchase a copy of Adams' book and carefully plan your itinerary. You can also get some good information by searching the Thompson River on the internet. Be forewarned: this is wild country - rugged, isolated and it's easy to get disoriented or lost here.

White Owl Falls

Stream: Thompson River   USGS Quad: Reid, NC, SC
Rating: excellent   Landowner: Nantahala National Forest
Type: cascade   Trail length: 0.2 mile (one way)
Height: 20 feet   Difficulty: moderate
Stream flow: medium   Elevation: 2,840 feet

Directions to the trailhead

From the intersection of U.S. 64 and Hwy. 281 in Sapphire take Hwy. 281 south for 3.7 miles. Park in the pull-off on the right side of the road. This pull-off is just a few hundred yards beyond Brewer Road (#1189) which is on the left side of the road.

White Owl Falls

Trail description

Walk across the road to the point where the guardrail begins. Step across the guardrail and walk approximately 40 yards (just before the utility lines) to the point where a path drops down the highway rip rap and enters the woods. Follow the overgrown but obvious path down to the waterfall. Though the path is short you will have to take your time as you descend to the base.

Description

Considering its proximity to the highway White Owl Falls is wonderfully secluded. Here the Thompson River plunges over a wide 20-foot ledge into a shallow plunge pool. The cascade fans across the rocky ledge covering nearly every square inch of the rock face when the water is high. The broad plunge pool is somewhat open and receives a good deal of sun which makes photography tricky. Be extremely careful around the base of the falls as the rocks are extremely slippery. I found out the hard way on a past visit.

High Falls

Stream: Thompson River   USGS Quad: Reid, NC, SC
Rating: excellent   Landowner: Nantahala National Forest
Type: steep waterslide   Trail length: 1.4 miles (one way)
Height: 60 feet   Difficulty: moderate (obscure trail junctions)
Stream flow: medium   Elevation: 2,760 feet

Directions to the trailhead

From the intersection of U.S. 64 and Hwy. 281 in Sapphire take Hwy. 281 south for 3.6 miles. Turn left onto Brewer Road (#1189) and park in the pull-off on the right side of the road.

Trail description

From the roadside parking area locate the old logging road that intersects at the corner of Hwy. 281 and Brewer Road. Follow this road uphill into the forest. At mile 0.65 pass a roadbed on the right. Continue straight ahead. At mile 0.85 you will pass a side path on the left. At mile 0.9 another old overgrown road veers off to the right. It's easy to miss so make sure you're looking for it. Veer right onto this roadbed and follow the path (which roughly parallels the Thompson River) though you cannot see the river at this point. Continue along the trail for about 0.4 mile and look for the side path that leads down to the falls. At one point there was a young poplar tree with lettering carved into it. You'll hear the waterfall long before you arrive at the side path. You may also find flagging or a small pile of stones to mark the path. Take the side trail down to a point below the main plunge pool.

High Falls -
Thompson River

Description

The best view of this magnificent waterfall is probably from the opposite side of the river, but that is a wet (and dangerous) proposition during normal to high water levels. High Falls is a real sleeper among the waterfalls of the area. It is quite unusual and undoubtedly beautiful as it flows smoothly over a steep river-wide ledge into a broad rock-laden plunge pool. Use a great deal of care as you maneuver around to get a good view of the waterfall. If you're here to photograph the waterfall you might have to get your feet wet in order to get a really good shot. Be very careful if you climb out at the top - the smooth rocks at the brink of the falls are deceptively steep and very slippery when wet. Better to play it safe and enjoy High Falls from the base.

Falls of the Horsepasture River

The Horsepasture River gets my vote for most interesting stream name and comes in second to none in terms of beauty and power. Back in 1986, a 4.5 mile section of this stunningly beautiful stream was placed under the protection of the Wild and Scenic Rivers Act. Good thing, because a few years earlier a 6-mile section of the river was nearly lost to the Carrasan Power Company of California who proposed to build a series of hydroelectric plants on the river.

For many years throngs of visitors parked along busy Hwy. 281 and descended to the river to enjoy its many waterfalls, particularly Drift Falls (Bust-Your-Butt), and the other major waterfalls downstream along a popular trail. In 1998 the owner of the quarry directly across the highway purchased the property containing Drift Falls and immediately closed access to the waterfall. Even more frustrating were the dozens of roadside "parking spots" that were lost. Park along Hwy. 281 now and you will receive a ticket - guaranteed.

Fortunately, Gorges State Park came into being around this time. In the last few years the park has made some tremendous improvements - including a new trailhead to the waterfalls on the Horsepasture. Interestingly, the falls now must be viewed in reverse order from how they were visited for so many years. Today you start at Rainbow Falls and work upriver to Turtleback. Consult the park for the latest information - things are changing fast at Gorges State Park.

Rainbow Falls ★

Stream: Horsepasture River	USGS Quad: Reid, NC, SC
Rating: spectacular	Landowner: Pisgah National Forest
Type: steep cascade	Trail length: 1.5 miles (one way)
Height: 125 feet	Difficulty: strenuous (elevation gain)
Stream flow: large	Elevation: 2,740 feet

Directions to the trailhead

From the intersection of U.S. 64 and Hwy. 281 in Sapphire take Hwy. 281 south for 0.9 mile. Turn left and follow the park loop road for 1.6 miles to the large parking area on the right.

Trail description

Old habits are hard to break. Tens of thousands of visitors over the years scrambled down the steep highway paths that accessed the rugged trail that followed the Horsepasture River downstream from Hwy. 281. Park here now and you'll absolutely be ticketed and maybe even towed. Thanks to the establishment of Gorges State Park in 1999 there is now an official trail that provides access to these wonderful waterfalls. The kicker is that it is now both a longer and a more strenuous hike.

From the Horsepasture Falls parking area in Gorges State Park proceed to the information boards at the lower end of the parking area. Enter the woods on a broad trail that has been constructed with a nice bed of crushed gravel. It follows an old roadbed downhill along a moderate gradient through a broad looping switchback into the Horsepasture Gorge. The trail exits the park boundary around mile 0.8, and the quality of the trail decreases a few steps as well. As you near the 1.1 mile point the trail comes alongside the Horsepasture River and crosses a moderate creek that hikers must either rock hop or balance on several small logs placed here by previous hikers.

Just beyond the creek enter and pass through a large primitive camping area. The path undulates up and down somewhat beyond the camping area and offers some great views of the cascading Horsepasture River as it weaves between massive boulders strewn across the gorge. Be sure to look for the prominent side path that drops down toward the distinct sound of falling waterfall. You're not at Rainbow yet; in this case it's Hidden Falls, a small but powerful ledge against the right bank. It's worth the slight detour.

The final 0.2 mile climbs steeply and the main viewing area for Rainbow Falls is actually an open stretch along the main hiking trail. It's in the waterfall's extensive spray zone so if the river is high you'll likely get a bit wet.

Rainbow Falls
- a beautiful display
of wildflowers is
often found along
the open trail at the
upper overlook.

Description

Rainbow Falls is definitely the most impressive of the Horsepasture's falls easily accessible to the public. The upper overlook provides an excellent view of the entire cascade from an elevation roughly equal to the brink of the falls. In the summer months an impressive display of wildflowers provides an excellent foreground for photographs as the cascade fills the right side of the enormous cliff.

This powerful waterfall has a healthy spray zone, and as the name suggests, rainbows can form when lighting conditions are just right. Moonbows, which are simply rainbows formed by moonlight, are also somewhat common here, although being out on a trail at night isn't wise (or legal in some parks). At high water levels the wind pattern created by the waterfall can carry drenching clouds of spray all the way up to the upper observation deck several hundred feet above the base of the waterfall. Everything seems to come together here to create one of the most beautiful waterfalls in the region. Catch it at its best and prepare your senses to be overwhelmed.

As Rainbow Falls booms over the enormous bedrock cliff, tons of falling water meets a protruding ledge sending an explosion of aerated water outward from the cliff. The water then recollects and plunges into a plunge pool surrounded by huge boulders and fragmented slabs of rock. The usual waterfall dangers are magnified even more than usual at Rainbow Falls. A perpetual shroud of mist keeps the rocks around the base slippery at all times.

I need to say a few words about the top of the waterfall as well. The brink of Rainbow Falls is open and easily accessible *and very dangerous*. There have been numerous fatalities from visitors trying to get too close to the brink for the dizzying look down. There are no railings here so stay away from the brink - especially if you have children. Other fatalities are attributed to persons swimming or wading in the pools between Rainbow Falls and Turtleback Falls. It is possible to get caught in the swift current and be swept to your death on this part of the river. Use good common sense and stay out of the river between these two waterfalls!

Turtleback Falls

Stream: Horsepasture River   USGS Quad: Reid, NC, SC
Rating: excellent   Landowner: Pisgah National Forest
Type: waterslide/free fall   Trail length: 1.7 miles (one way)
Height: 10 feet   (0.2 mile beyond Rainbow Falls)
Stream flow: large   Difficulty: strenuous
    Elevation: 2,765 feet

Directions to the trailhead

Follow the directions to the Gorges State Park and the Rainbow Falls Trail on page 138.

Trail description

Beyond Rainbow Falls the trail climbs slightly before leveling out for several hundred yards as it approaches Turtleback Falls. It's a fairly easy walk from Rainbow to Turtleback and it would be a shame to come this far and not invest the minimal effort in time and energy to view the Horsepasture River's next big feature attraction.

Turtleback Falls

Description

Turtleback is a fascinating waterfall considering its relatively small size. Its name is appropriate as the shape definitely resembles a turtle's shell. It's also sometimes called *Umbrella Falls* - understandable as well. Though only about 10 feet high the plunge attracts thrill seekers who slide over the curved drop and launch into mid-air momentarily before hitting the pool at the base known as the "Chug Hole." There have been drownings here; the current is strong and rocks around the waterfall are slick. Be aware of the risks. It's also a great spot for photos as the waterfall can be shot from several angles. The rocks directly across from the waterfall provide a nice "head on" vantage point.

Drift Falls

Stream: Horsepasture River   USGS Quad: Reid, NC, SC
Rating: excellent   Landowner: private property
Type: steep waterslide   Trail length: 1.8 miles (one way)
Height: 30 feet   Difficulty: strenuous
Stream flow: large   Elevation: 2,800 feet

Directions to the trailhead
        Follow the directions to the Gorges State Park and the Rainbow Falls Trail on page 138.

Trail description
        From Turtleback Falls continue along the riverside trail as it makes a looping turn around the falls and walk several hundred yards upstream to the signs and barricades which announce the end of the road (so to speak). From this point forward this is private property and you had better respect it! According to *North Carolina Waterfalls* author Kevin Adams' research, the property owner's boundary line runs across the pool. Work your way to the river's edge and up as far as the signs but BE SURE to stay on the National Forest property.

Drift Falls - a photo from the early 1990s

Description
        Hundreds of daredevils once took the plunge over Drift Falls' steep shoulders into its huge plunge pool. Though you can't get close you can still get *close enough* to appreciate the power and beauty of this magnificent waterfall from downstream. If the water is normal to low it rushes in almost hushed tones over the massive dome of granite. If you catch it after a heavy or flooding rain the tremendous cloud of spray may obscure the falls entirely.

Stairway Falls

Stream: Horsepasture River
Rating: excellent
Type: multi-level cascade
Height: 50 feet
Stream flow: large

USGS Quad: Reid, NC, SC
Landowner: Pisgah National Forest
Trail length: 1 mile (one way)
Difficulty: moderate to strenuous
Elevation: 2,400 feet

Directions to the trailhead
Follow the directions to the Gorges State Park and the Rainbow Falls Trail on page 138.

Trail description
Stairway Falls is about 0.8 mile downstream of Rainbow Falls so hikers on the Rainbow Falls Trail pass relatively close. Unfortunately there aren't any signs in place to direct you to the falls so if you choose to visit you have to find your way. One web source claims that as you near the primitive campsite (coming from the parking area) there is a sign that directs you to Rainbow Falls. This source states there is a path starting here that leads down to the falls. I have never gone this route so I cannot confirm this. However, I have been via the "old" route: returning from Rainbow Falls walk 0.4 to the primitive campsite along the trail. Cross the creek and about 20 or so yards beyond it locate a primitive path that descends to another primitive camping area not far from the brink of the falls. In general follow the most prominent paths toward the sound of falling water - I won't be more specific because the area has changed quite a bit over the last few years. Expect that these paths will be rough and could generally have quite a few deadfalls across them.

Description
Stairway Falls possesses its own distinct personality which is completely different from the three previous Horsepasture waterfalls. Six individual ledges in quick succession create this appropriately named waterfall. There is a nice vantage point at the far end of the wide plunge pool across from the waterfall. This spot gives visitors a view of at least 5 of the ledges one above another. Visit Stairway at any time other than a busy weekend and you may have this location all to yourself.
This is the end of the line for novice waterfall enthusiasts. Windy Falls, the wildest and most dangerous of the Horsepasture's falls, is just a few miles downstream, but it is both difficult and dangerous to reach and view. Refer back to Kevin Adams' book *North Carolina Waterfalls* for a complete description of this very dangerous section of the river.

Falls of Gorges State Park

It's hard to believe but this little-known park is the only North Carolina state park west of Asheville. Created in 1999, over 7,000 acres of pristine forest are now protected within the confines of the park; another 2,900 acres is managed by the North Carolina Wildlife Resorces Commission. Because it is relatively new (and created during a perod of shrinking state budgets no doubt) the park has developed slowly and as of yet offers little in the way of facilities. Perform a web search for Gorges State Park or obtain a copy of *The North Carolina Sierra Club's Guide to Jocassee Gorges* by Bill Thomas for more information on this fascinating area.

As far as waterfalls go there are plenty to be explored at Gorges but because access within the park is difficult, many of the falls simply require more effort than the novice waterfall enthusiast will wish to expend (such as those requiring hiking long distances and/or bushwhacking). This guidebook will stick to those that are relatively safe and simple to access.

Bearwallow Falls

Stream: Bearwallow Creek
Rating: good
Type: steep cascade
Height: 50 feet upper drop
Stream flow: small

USGS Quad: Reid, NC, SC
Landowner: Gorges State Park
Trail length: .75 miles (one way)
Difficulty: moderate to strenuous
Elevation: 2,880 feet

Directions to the trailhead

From the intersection of U.S. 64 and Hwy. 281 in Sapphire take Hwy. 281 south for 0.9 mile. Turn left into the park and drive approximately one mile to the closed parking area that is the site of the proposed visitor center. Turn left here and proceed about one more additional mile to the Bearwallow Falls and Bearwallow Valley Overlook trailheads.

Trail description

This trail has changed a good bit since I last hiked it. Construction of the new park loop road has forced the relocation of the trailhead closer to the falls. This is a good thing since the waterfall isn't the most impressive you'll see in this region. Follow the blue triangles from the parking area for about three-quarters of a mile. The last portion of the trail drops rather dramatically down to an observation deck overlooking the falls. The park literature describes it as strenuous. I would probably go more with *moderate* but either way it's a nice hike in a beautiful natural setting.

Description

    Compared to some of the other waterfalls in this section, Bearwallow Falls might be considered less than dramatic. If you invest 1.5 miles in a destination you might want a bigger payoff. Unfortunately much of Bearwallow Falls is hidden beneath a thick shroud of streamside foliage. In fact the beautiful upper cascades are hidden completely. From the look of things plenty of people strike out on their own and bushwhack down to the waterfall for a better view, but this is certainly not recommended and definitely not something the park would approve of. The location of the observation deck leaves much to be desired, so consider this hike carefully before committing several hours of your time.

Toxaway Falls

Stream: Toxaway River
Rating: excellent
Type: steep cascades/waterslides
Height: 150 feet
Stream flow: large

USGS Quad: Reid, NC,SC
Landowner: Gorges State Park
Trail length: roadside
Difficulty: n/a
Elevation: 2,920 feet

Directions to the trailhead

    From the intersection of U.S. 64 and Hwy. 281 in Sapphire follow U.S. 64 east for 2.2 miles to the pull-off on the east side of the bridge.

Trail description

    There's a good bit of development around this wonderful waterfall that detracts from its beauty but it's still hard to pass up an escarpment waterfall located right alongside a busy highway. You can get a decent view from here but only of the upper cascade. The good news is that Gorges State Park now owns the land on the east side of the falls (and a narrow sliver on the west side as well) so the adventurous can drop down the scramble paths to get better views from various points along the way.

    The base of the upper drop isn't much of a challenge but to reach the bottom of the entire run is much more difficult. The only way you can get a view from the other side of the waterfall without trespassing is to descend to the base, cross the river, then climb the west bank. But wading a river is not recommended at any time (and the view isn't really much better anyway).

    Toxaway Falls is an extraordinarily beautiful waterfall but the encroachment of highway bridges and condominiums definitely mars the beauty of the area.

This beautiful area is also rich in history. Much like Tallulah Falls to the south, Toxaway was once a resort destination that attracted the rich and influential. Also like Tallulah Falls a "disaster" led to its downfall. In July, 1916, a series of hurricanes hit western North Carolina and caused extensive flooding. One month later another hurricane drenched the area with nearly two feet of rain. On August 13, 1916, Lake Toxaway's earthen dam above the waterfall collapsed and millions of gallons of water from the lake raced down the gorge ripping away streamside vegetation and exposing bedrock for nearly two miles downstream. With the dam and 600+ acre lake gone, the popular Toxaway Inn closed. The area fell into relative obscurity. In 1960 however, the Lake Toxaway Company acquired the property and rebuilt the lake. Today it is one of North Carolina's largest private lakes and is home to hundreds of magnificent upscale homes.

The Falls of Panthertown Valley

Magnificent Panthertown Valley is tucked away just north of scenic Hwy. 64 between Cashiers and Sapphire. The valley was once a little-known destination for hunters and fishermen but it is anything but little-known today boasting an impressive collection of granite cliffs, pristine streams and a growing system of hiking trails. Partly because of its prominent bare rock cliffs it has gained the nickname of the "Yosemite of the East." Quite an overstatement but ever since the 6,300-acre valley became a component of the Nantahala National Forest in the late 1980s it has been growing in popularity.

Hikers, campers, mountain bikers and trout fishermen are the primary benefactors of Panthertown's beauty. A number of pristine streams flow through the confines of Panthertown Valley. The mighty Tuckaseegee is born high on the valley's forested slopes and is fed by streams with names such as Frolictown, Panthertown and Greenland. Because of its dramatic geology, several impressive waterfalls are found here as well. Five of these falls are included in this section. None of these should be too difficult to find and all make nice day hike destinations.

While there is plenty of hiking for the average Joe, there are trails and destinations in the valley best left to the super-fit and advanced hiker. Some of these destinations like the Bonas Defeat Trail along the Tuckasegee River require some climbing or bouldering skills and cover challenging terrain with a risk of flash flooding. Be sure you investigate your destination before setting off in Panthertown Valley.

Although the current trail system in Pantertown Valley is light years ahead of just a few years back it can still be a confusing area. Slickrock Expeditions in Cullowhee offers an excellent resource called *A Guide's Guide to Panthertown Valley*. This topographical map includes the logging roads and trail network in the valley. The maps are sold at many outfitters stores in the area or visit www.slickrockexpeditions.com to obtain a copy.

There are two main entrances into the valley. The western access point can be reached from Cashiers while the eastern access point is in the Lake Toxaway area. Although either entrance is acceptable please note that mileage distances and directions are given from the closer of the two access points.

While only a handful of the valley's waterfalls are detailed here, many more can be visited if you obtain a copy of the Panthertown Valley map and study it thoroughly. The ones I have listed here are fairly close to the entrances and don't require getting much more than a mile from your vehicle. I definitely would not recommend exploring Panthertown Valley without a detailed up-to-date map.

Schoolhouse Falls ★

Stream: Greenland Creek
Rating: excellent
Type: free-fall
Height: 20 feet
Stream flow: medium

USGS Quad: Big Ridge, NC
Landowner: Nantahala National Forest
Trail length: 1.2 miles (one way)
Difficulty: moderate
Elevation: 3,670 feet

Directions to the trailhead

To reach Panthertown Valley's eastern entrance: From the intersection of U.S. 64 and NC 281 east of the Toxaway River bridge take NC 281 north for 0.8 mile. Fork left onto Cold Mountain Road (the road sign is actually on the right side of the road). Follow the road for 5.6 miles to the gap. Continue as the road curves sharply left and drive an additional 0.2 mile. Turn right and proceed several hundred yards to a gate and small dirt parking area.

Trail description

Enter the woods on the Panthertown Valley Trail that begins to the right of the gate. It leads to the old access road. Turn left and follow the road as it begins a gradual descent. At mile 0.6 there is a prominent social path on the left that descends to the top of Schoolhouse Falls but this is not the desired route. The easier way is to continue on the road to the next intersection. Bear left and cross the footbridge over Greenland Creek. Turn left again and walk several hundred yards upstream to the waterfall.

Schoolhouse Falls

Description

      Schoolhouse Falls is Panthertown Valley's best known cascade. This beautiful waterfall plunges over an overhanging ledge into a magnificent open plunge pool. A scramble path actually goes behind the drop and provides an amazing vantage point. An old schoolhouse, built for the children of loggers who worked the valley in the 1920s, was built near the waterfall. The story goes that bad economic times of the Depression ended the logging before the schoolhouse ever held classes.

Greenland Creek Falls ★

Stream: Greenland Creek   USGS Quad: Lake Toxaway, NC
Rating: excellent   Landowner: Nantahala National Forest
Type: steep cascade   Trail length: 1.0 mile (one way)
Height: 45 feet   Difficulty: moderate
Stream flow: medium   Elevation: 3,880 feet

Directions to the trailhead

      Follow the directions to the eastern entrance of Panthertown Valley on page 148. Turn onto the parking access road and drive up to the Mac's Gap Trail marker on the left. The trail begins here.

Trail description

      The Mac's Gap Trail follows an old logging road into the valley passing underneath a power line around 0.2 mile. Continue to mile 0.7 to a

Greenland Creek Falls

a junction just before the creek crossing. Look for the Greenland Creek Trail to the left. It's a bit overgrown and winds through a thick rhododendron thicket. It steps across a few small creeks before reaching the waterfall in about 0.3 mile. To get the best view of this cascade you may have to rock hop or wade into the stream. Note: if you have a Panthertown Valley map you may have noticed a social trail that runs from Schoolhouse Falls south. My advice is to avoid this path as it leaves much to be desired on its southern end.

Description
        This beautiful waterfall tumbles in two primary stages into a small rock-laden plunge pool. The upper cascades push against the left bank onto a flat, protruding ledge while the shorter lower series primarily hugs the right bank. This waterfall is quite beautiful and usually exceeds expectations.

Granny Burrell Falls

Stream: Panthertown Creek   USGS Quad: Big Ridge, NC
Rating: good   Landowner: Nantahala National Forest
Type: waterslide   Trail length: 1.3 miles (one way)
Height: 15 feet   Difficulty: moderate
Stream flow: medium   Elevation: 3,680 feet

Directions to the trailhead
        To reach Panthertown Valley's western entrance: From the intersection of U.S. 64 and NC 107 in Cashiers follow U.S. 64 east for 1.9 miles. Turn left onto Cedar Creek Road (1120). Follow Cedar Creek Road for 2.2 miles. Turn right onto Breedlove Road (1121). Proceed along Breedlove for 3.3 miles at which point the road becomes gravel. Continue an additional 0.3 mile to a compact parking area and gated trailhead.

Trail description
        From the gated trailhead at the western end of the valley follow the Panthertown Valley Trail (PVT) for 0.3 mile to Salt Rock, an open overlook which provides a scenic view of the valley. At 0.6 mile the road reaches a fork. Turn left and continue descending until you reach a 3-way intersection (The PVT continues straight ahead to Panthertown's eastern access point). Turn right here and walk through a primitive camping area and then through a thick grove of white pine until you come to a footbridge spanning Panthertown Creek. Continue 50 yards beyond the bridge and take the trail to the right. Follow the path for about 0.1 mile upstream to the falls.

Trail description

Granny Burrell is not a major waterfall by any means but it has developed a following as a popular spot for summer visitors who slide on the smooth rocks below the falls and swim in the cascade's broad open pool. Not sure if Granny Burrell frequented the falls but the slide is so gentle she probably could have.

Granny Burrell Falls

Falls on Frolictown Creek

Stream: Panthertown Creek
Rating: good
Type: steep cascade
Height: 15 feet
Stream flow: small

USGS Quad: Big Ridge, NC
Landowner: Nantahala National Forest
Trail length: 1.0 mile (one way)
Difficulty: moderate
Elevation: 3,710 feet

Directions to the trailhead

Follow the directions on page 150 to Panthertown Valley's western entrance.

Trail description

From the gated trailhead at the western end of the valley follow the Panthertown Valley Trail for 0.3 mile to Salt Rock, an open overlook which provides a scenic view of Panthertown Valley. At 0.6 mile the road reaches a fork (The road to the left goes to Granny Burrell Falls). Turn right here and proceed about 0.25 mile to a clearing. Stay along the right edge of the clearing and begin a gradual descent to a ford on Frolictown Creek at the 1 mile point. Just before reaching the ford look for a short side path on the left that drops to the base of this pretty cascade.

Wilderness Falls

Stream: Frolictown Creek tributary
Rating: excellent
Type: steep waterslide
Height: 70 feet
Stream flow: small

USGS Quad: Big Ridge, NC
Landowner: Nantahala National Forest
Trail length: 1.4 miles (one way)
Difficulty: moderate
Elevation: 3,800 feet

Directions to the trailhead

Follow the previous directions to Panthertown Valley's western entrance.

Trail description

This waterfall is a perfect companion destination after visiting the falls on Frolictown Creek on the previous page. Proceed to Frolictown Creek. When you reach the ford instead of taking the side path to the left that drops to the waterfall, turn right and take the Wilderness Falls Trail on the opposite side of the road. It's a fairly easy 0.4 mile walk to the waterfall. As you get close you will have to scramble down to the base of this steep waterslide in order to view it.

At high water levels Wilderness Falls is particularly beautiful. As you near the waterfall the path turns and follows the creek upstream to this open waterslide. You can short cut back to Salt Rock by continuing on this trail for another 0.4 mile. It climbs very steeply at first until it reaches the top of Wilderness Falls then the grade eases up until you reach the Panthertown Valley Trail between Salt Rock and the western entrance.

falls on Frolictown Creek tributary

North Carolina Hub #3 - Rosman & Brevard

see introduction on next page

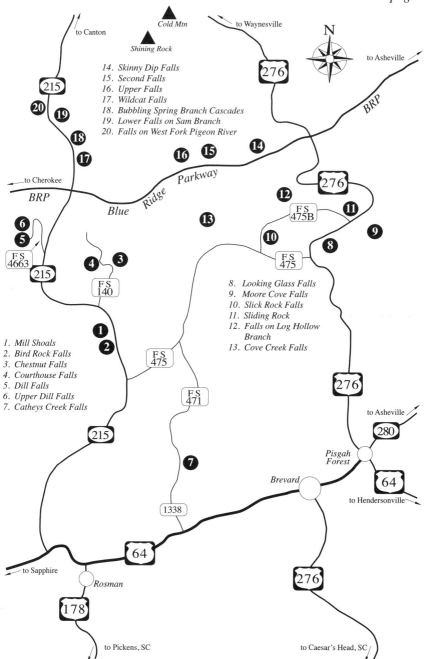

to Canton

Cold Mtn

Shining Rock

to Waynesville

N

to Asheville

215

20 19

18

17

14. *Skinny Dip Falls*
15. *Second Falls*
16. *Upper Falls*
17. *Wildcat Falls*
18. *Bubbling Spring Branch Cascades*
19. *Lower Falls on Sam Branch*
20. *Falls on West Fork Pigeon River*

276

BRP

to Cherokee

BRP

Blue

Ridge

Parkway

16 15 14

276

12

FS 475B

11

13

10

FS 475

8

9

6

5

FS 4663

215

4 3

FS 140

8. *Looking Glass Falls*
9. *Moore Cove Falls*
10. *Slick Rock Falls*
11. *Sliding Rock*
12. *Falls on Log Hollow Branch*
13. *Cove Creek Falls*

1 2

FS 475

1. *Mill Shoals*
2. *Bird Rock Falls*
3. *Chestnut Falls*
4. *Courthouse Falls*
5. *Dill Falls*
6. *Upper Dill Falls*
7. *Catheys Creek Falls*

FS 471

276

to Asheville

280

215

7

Pisgah Forest

Brevard

64

to Hendersonville

1338

276

64

to Sapphire

Rosman

178

to Pickens, SC

to Caesar's Head, SC

North Carolina Hub #3 - Rosman & Brevard

This hub can easily be subdivided into two or three smaller hubs for an afternoon of waterfall watching - for instance, the Hwy. 215 falls north of Rosman; the U.S. 276 falls north of Brevard; the cascades of the Blue Ridge Parkway and those along Hwy. 215 north of the Parkway. There are definitely a wide variety of waterfalls and waterfall experiences to be enjoyed in and around Rosman and Brevard. The area around Pisgah Forest features some of the most visited waterfalls in the southern Appalachians, including beauties such as Looking Glass Falls and those on the Blue Ridge Parkway at Graveyard Fields. Others offer a delightful wilderness experience far from the crowds.

For a taste of civilization in the mountains it's hard to beat the friendly town of Brevard. The quaint downtown offers a nice variety of shoppes and restaurants. If you want to find out more about the history of the magnificent forests in and around Brevard and Pisgah Forest be sure to venture north along U.S. 276 to the Cradle of Forestry.

Mill Shoals ★

Stream: North Fork French Broad
   River & Shoal Creek
Rating: excellent
Type: free fall; steep cascade
Height: 15 feet
Stream flow: large

USGS Quad: Rosman, NC
Landowner: Living Waters Ministry
Trail length: short walk
Difficulty: easy
Elevation: 2,760 feet

Directions to the trailhead

From the intersection of U.S. 64 and NC 215 north of Rosman proceed north on NC 215 for 7.6 miles. Just before you reach the Living Waters Ministry there is a small pull-off along the highway that is currently marked by a small pile of rocks. Park here.

Description

It's not clearly evident as you view them from downstream but the two waterfalls visible here occur on different streams. The stream on the right, Shoal Creek, tumbles over a series of steep cascades and enters the North Fork of the French Broad River. Together the cascades are known simply as Mill Shoals. Just a few yards to the left the North Fork French Broad plunges over

a 15-foot sheer drop into a wide plunge pool. The larger falls has also been
known over the years as French Broad Falls.

This is yet another location where a private landowner (in this case a
ministry) allows continuing access to a beautiful waterfall. Treat the area with
care and don't do anything stupid to endanger the access we currently enjoy.
Keep the area free of litter and use good etiquette. It's always a good idea to
ask for permission just in case the owner's change their minds about allowing
access to the area.

Mill Shoals

Bird Rock Falls

Stream: North Fork French Broad River

Rating: excellent

Type: steep cascade

Height: 15 feet

Stream flow: large

USGS Quad: Rosman, NC

Landowner: Living Waters Ministry

Trail length: 0.2 mile (one way)

Difficulty: easy to moderate

Elevation: 2,720 feet

Directions to the trailhead

Follow the directions on the previous page to Mill Shoals.

Description

From Mill Shoals follow the riverside trail about 300 yards downstream to Bird Rock Falls. Although you pass a number of pretty cascades
along the way, a massive grey cliff rising above the opposite stream bank
verifies that you have arrived at the correct destination. The waterfall isn't
particularly large but its location below the massive overhanging bluff creates a
beautifully unique wilderness setting, especially when the river is high and the
flow covers most of the ledge.

A side trail drops down to the brink of the falls, while the main path
continues down to the base. The rocks are very slippery when wet so be very

careful. The bluff seems to amplify the roar of the falling water and the presence of so much exposed rock creates an almost reverent setting. Appropriately, the camp calls the cascade Cathedral Falls.

Bird Rock Falls

Chestnut Falls

Stream: Chestnut Creek
Rating: good
Type: cascade
Height: 20 feet
Stream flow: small

USGS Quad: Sam Knob, NC
Landowner: Pisgah National Forest
Trail length: 0.9 mile (one way)
Difficulty: moderate
Elevation: 3,720 feet

Directions to the trailhead

From the intersection of U.S. 64 and NC 215 north of Rosman proceed north on NC 215 for 10.3 miles. Turn right onto FS 140 (Courthouse Creek Road) and proceed 2.6 miles to the gated road on the right (Kiesee Creek Road). Park here (be careful not to block the gate). *Note:* FS 140 can be fairly rough in spots and might not be suitable for low-clearance vehicles.

Trail description

Follow Kiesee Creek Road into the woods. At 0.8 mile, just prior to reaching a fork, turn left onto a path that enters a primitive camping area along the creek. Continue upstream to the cascade. This waterfall isn't the most scenic in the area and it is difficult to take a really good photograph without getting a lot of downed trees or branches in the way; but it is still a pretty hike. The waterfall was named in remembrance of the American chestnut tree, once a stately member of the southern Appalachian forest community but wiped out by an Asian fungus introduced early in the 20th century.

Courthouse Falls

Stream: Courthouse Creek   USGS Quad: Sam Knob, NC
Rating: excellent   Landowner: Pisgah National Forest
Type: steep waterslide   Trail length: 0.35 mile (one way)
Height: 40 feet   Difficulty: moderate
Stream flow: small/medium   Elevation: 3,340 feet

Directions to the trailhead

From the intersection of U.S. 64 and NC 215 north of Rosman proceed
north on NC 215 for 10.3 miles. Turn right onto FS 140 (Courthouse Creek
Road) and proceed 3 miles to the Courthouse Creek crossing. Park in the pull-
off on the right side of the road beyond the creek crossing.

Description

From the roadside parking area follow the Summy Cove Trail
alongside Courthouse Creek downstream on an old logging road for 0.25 mile
to a point where you can glimpse the waterfall through the underbrush to the
left. Continue along the main trail to a prominent side path on the left that
drops down to the river opposite the waterfall's beautiful emerald-green plunge
pool. The powerful cascade rockets through a narrow cleft carved into solid
bedrock. At high water levels it is quite a show. Swimmers occasionally test
the waters of the plunge pool, but be forewarned: the creek is *painfully* cold
even in the hot summer months and the
current is very strong at the head of the
pool underneath the waterfall.

The name Courthouse Falls
is said to originate from the Cherokee
legend Judculla who, according to
legend, held council in a nearby cave.
Courthouse Creek forms below the
Devils Courthouse, a 5,720-foot rock
precipice that is prominently visible
as you travel along this portion of the
Blue Ridge Parkway.

Courthouse Falls

Dill Falls

Stream: Tanasee Creek
Rating: excellent
Type: free-fall/steep cascade
Height: 60 feet
Stream flow: small

USGS Quad: Sam Knob, NC
Landowner: Pisgah National Forest
Trail length: 0.8 mile (one way)
Difficulty: moderate
Elevation: 4,180 feet

Directions to the trailhead

From the intersection of U.S. 64 and NC 215 north of Rosman proceed north on NC 215 for 14 miles. Turn left onto FS 4663. Continue 1.8 miles (do not go right at mile 0.5) to the point where FS 4663B bears left. It would probably be best to park here as FS 4663B can be very bumpy. Note: FS 4663 may be gated at the 0.6 mile point due to past flood damage; this would add 1.2 miles to your hike.

Trail description

Hike FS 4663B for 0.6 mile to a junction where the road splits 3 ways. One heads straight ahead and begins climbing and one goes far right; the one you want to take runs between the two and begins descending. Follow it for about 0.2 mile to a point where the road makes a wet crossing of splashing Tanasee Creek. Walk upstream to the base of the waterfall. This pretty cascade tumbles gracefully over a steep rock ledge into a boulder-studded pool.

Upper Dill Falls, a nice 25-foot falls upstream of Dill Falls is also worth a look. Return to the junction featuring the 3-way split and take the road to the far right. Climb steeply for a few hundred yards then proceed along the trail as it passes high above the waterfall. Descend the steep bank along a scramble path to view the waterfall from the base.

Looking Glass Falls ★

Stream: Looking Glass Creek
Rating: excellent
Type: free-fall
Height: 60 feet
Stream flow: medium

USGS Quad: Shining Rock, NC
Landowner: Pisgah National Forest
Trail length: roadside
Difficulty: n/a
Elevation: 2,360 feet

Directions to the trailhead

From the intersection of U.S. 64, U.S. 276 and NC 280 east of downtown Brevard proceed north of U.S. 276 for 5.5 miles to an extended pull-off on the right. If you are coming from the north this parking area is located 9.2 miles south of the Blue Ridge Parkway.

Description

Looking Glass Falls is without doubt the most well-known and heavily visited waterfall in the area, and it's little wonder. This beautiful free-falling waterfall is prominently visible from busy U.S. 276 and is just a short drive from two of the area's most popular attractions - Sliding Rock and The Cradle of Forestry. It is rare in these parts that a free-falling cascade of this size occurs on a stream so easily accessible. It's a great combination: tons of water, a beautiful pool and a rugged cliff.

The view is great from the parking area but head down an easy set of stairs and you'll be face-to-face with this powerful juggernaut. The creek and waterfall are named for nearby Looking Glass Rock, a rare granite dome popular with hikers and rock climbers.

Looking Glass Falls

Cathey's Creek Falls

Stream: Cathey's Creek
Rating: excellent
Type: long cascades
Height: 50 feet
Stream flow: medium

USGS Quad: Rosman, NC
Landowner: Pisgah National Forest
Trail length: 100 yards (one way)
Difficulty: steep scramble
Elevation: 2,520 feet

Directions to the trailhead
From Brevard take U.S. 64 west for 3.3 miles and turn right at the sign for Kuykendall Group Camp. Make a quick left onto Cathey's Creek Road and proceed 3.3 miles to the pull off. Note Cathey's Creek Road is paved for the first 0.7 mile - after that prepare to bounce a bit as it becomes gravel.

Trail description
There are several primitive paths that drop down to the waterfall and none is particularly easy. You'll definitely want to have your hands free to hold on to the rhododenron limbs as you descend to the creek. This long series of cascades is quite scenic but a bit frustrating to view as it is much longer than it is high, and finding a really good vantage point may take a bit of work. According to *The Land of Waterfalls* by Jim Bob Tinsley, the creek is named for a revolutionary war captain, George Cathey, who was awarded land in the area for his service in the war. The waterfall has also been known as High Falls in the past.

Moore Cove Falls

Stream: Moore Creek
Rating: excellent
Type: free-fall
Height: 50 feet
Stream flow: small

USGS Quad: Shining Rock, NC
Landowner: Pisgah National Forest
Trail length: 0.7 mile (one way)
Difficulty: easy
Elevation: 2,800 feet

Directions to the trailhead
From the intersection of U.S. 64, U.S. 276 and NC 280 east of downtown Brevard proceed north of U.S. 276 for 6.6 miles (1.4 miles beyond Looking Glass Falls). Pull into the small parking area to the right just before the highway bridge spanning Looking Glass Creek.

Trail and description

The trail begins on the upper end of the parking area adjacent to the highway bridge. Cross Looking Glass Creek over a recently constructed footbridge and closely follow the trail upstream as it zigzags across the creek several times. This pretty waterfall occurs in a tiny watershed and can all but disappear when the creek drops. To be quite frank when the creek is high the waterfall is still fairly small.

The most interesting feature of Moore Cove Falls is that it is yet another waterfall in the area that plunges over a recessed ledge; this creates a large dry space behind the tiny cascade that provides a unique perspective. The hike back into the beautiful cove is quite scenic also, offering something noteworthy at every time of year with fantastic spring wildflower displays, phenomenal fall color and ice formations in the cold winter months. I've never been disappointed in the scenery here, but I've also never gotten a really good photo of the waterfall. Moore Cove Falls is one of those attractions that just looks much better in person than it does on paper (or a computer screen).

Slick Rock Falls

Stream: Slick Rock Creek
Rating: good
Type: free-fall
Height: 30 feet
Stream flow: small

USGS Quad: Shining Rock, NC
Landowner: Pisgah National Forest
Trail length: 100 yards
Difficulty: easy
Elevation: 2,640 feet

Directions to the trailhead

From the intersection of U.S. 64, U.S. 276 and NC 280 east of downtown Brevard proceed north of U.S. 276 for 5.2 miles. Turn left onto FS 475 and proceed 1.5 miles, passing the entrance to the Pisgah Fish Hatchery and the Pisgah Center for Wildlife Eduation. Turn right onto FS 475B and proceed 1.1 miles to a sharp left bend in the road. Park here in the small pull-off.

Description

This pull-off accesses a Looking Glass Rock trailhead. Ascend the stairs and continue past the information board. In 50 yards take the trail fork to the right up to the base of this pretty free-falling cascade. The ledge which forms the waterfall, like many in this area, is recessed and the water spills into a fragmented rock pile at the base. The name originated from the dangerous conditions which occurs around the top of any waterfall, the expected result of smooth rocks and water. Seriously, even though it's not a big drop - the top of this waterfall is easily accessible and quite dangerous. The stream is fairly small and the waterfall diminishes greatly in prolonged dry conditions.

Sliding Rock ★

Stream: Looking Glass Creek
Rating: excellent
Type: long shallow slide
Height: approx. 20 feet
Stream flow: medium

USGS Quad: Shining Rock, NC
Landowner: Pisgah National Forest
Trail length: roadside
Difficulty: easy
Elevation: approx. 2,900 feet

Directions

From the intersection of U.S. 64, U.S. 276 and NC 280 east of downtown Brevard in Pisgah Forest proceed north of U.S. 276 for 7.6 miles. Turn left into the large parking area at Sliding Rock. There is a nominal fee of $1 per person to slide (except for young children).

Description

There are only a handful of waterfalls in this guidebook that you can actually ride and this one ranks with Sliding Rock in Tallulah Gorge as one of the best. Unlike Tallulah Gorge and its strict 100 person per day limit, hundreds if not thousands of people per day come to this Sliding Rock to take the thrilling ride down this 11,000 gallon per minute conveyor of icy, rushing water.

Sliding Rock - without the buildings and railings

Purists will scoff at its inclusion as a waterfall, but so what? It's not only thrilling, it's also quite beautiful. In the summer it may be darn near impossible to enjoy its scenic beauty with hundreds of sliders and gawkers crowding the scene. In the cooler months you can actually photograph the waterfall in its natural state as Looking Glass Creek fans across the smooth rock dome in a thin veneer of dancing water. The parking area has been greatly expanded over the years but it can still be difficult to find a space if you come at peak times. In other words, if you're coming to slide either come early in the day or expect to wait your turn for this classic Looking Glass Creek adventure.

Waterfall on Log Hollow Branch ★

Stream: Log Hollow Branch
Rating: excellent
Type: steep cascade
Height: 30 feet
Stream flow: small

USGS Quad: Shining Rock, NC
Landowner: Pisgah National Forest
Trail length: 0.5 mile (one way)
Difficulty: easy
Elevation: 3,280 feet

Directions to the trailhead

From the intersection of U.S. 64, U.S. 276 and NC 280 east of downtown Brevard in Pisgah Forest proceed north on U.S. 276 for 10.2 miles (4.6 miles south of the Blue Ridge Parkway). Turn left onto FS 475B (Headwaters Road) and proceed 1.6 miles. At this point you will come to a sharp left curve in the road. Park on the outside of the curve marked by a forest management sign.

Trail description

There is a gated logging road in the outside of the curve here. Follow this roadbed for just over 0.2 mile to a wooden footbridge over the creek. Continue on the old road to a second bridge. Follow the path across the bridge and up to the base. This is a surprisingly pretty waterfall at normal to high water levels and very well worth the minimal effort required to reach it.

Yet another waterfall on a southern tributary of Log Hollow Branch is less than a half-mile further. To reach it continue on the old logging road for about 0.45 mile and you'll meet the 60-foot combination free-fall and cascading drop face-to-face as it drops nearly onto the road. Don't bother going to the second waterfall if the first is low. Save your time and come again when conditions are favorable.

Cove Creek Falls ★

Stream: Cove Creek
Rating: excellent
Type: steep cascade
Height: 50 feet
Stream flow: small

USGS Quad: Shining Rock, NC
Landowner: Pisgah National Forest
Trail length: 1.25 miles (one way)
Difficulty: moderate
Elevation: 2,800 feet

Directions to the trailhead

From the intersection of U.S. 64, U.S. 276 and NC 280 east of downtown Brevard in Pisgah Forest proceed north on U.S. 276 for 5.2 miles. Turn left onto FS 475 and proceed 3.2 miles. There is a parking area on the left immediately preceding the bridge over Cove Creek. Note: FS 475 may not be open beyond the Pisgah Center for Wildlife Education.

Trail directions

There are a number of trails in this area, so be sure you follow directions precisely or you'll end up somewhere highly scenic, but it won't be Cove Creek Falls. Leave the parking area cross FS 475; begin walking up Forest Road #809. In approximately 140 yards turn right onto a side path which crosses the creek on a footbridge then angles back out to the road. Just beyond the 0.3 mile point the road passes a small cascade on the right. At mile 0.4, just before you reach the lower camping area, you will come to the Caney Bottom Loop Trail on the left. Turn onto this trail and follow a small creek upstream for about 120 yards. Turn right onto a prominent path that crosses this creek. Continue along the edge of the group camp. Approximately 0.3 mile beyond the small creek crossing you'll come to an intersection. The Caney Bottom Trail goes to the right; instead, continue straight on the Cove Creek Trail for about 0.35 mile to a side path on the right just past a small hemlock tree featuring yellow blazes. Walk up this path for several hundred yards to the cascade.

Description

This is a surprisingly scenic cascade. The surroundings are beautiful and it's far enough off the beaten path to make it feel like a true wilderness waterfall. Cove Creek Falls seems to become larger each time I visit it. With a good stream flow it is a real beauty as it cascades down a large multi-tiered ledge. Familiarize yourself with the trail network; the Cove Creek Trail and Caney Bottom Trails offer nice loop options which could extend your hike. The Caney Bottom Trail features some nice cascades and a few smaller falls as well.

Skinny Dip Falls ★

Stream: Yellowstone Prong East Fork Pigeon River
Rating: excellent
Type: steep cascade
Height: 30 feet
Stream flow: medium

USGS Quad: Shining Rock, NC
Landowner: Blue Ridge Parkway
Trail length: 0.4 mile (one way)
Difficulty: moderate
Elevation: 4,400 feet

Directions to the trailhead

The trailhead is located at the Looking Glass Rock Overlook at milepost 417 on the Blue Ridge Parkway. From the intersection of U.S. 276 and the Blue Ridge Parkway follow the parkway south for several miles to the overlook on the left.

Trail directions

From the Looking Glass Rock overlook walk to the northern end of the parking area and cross the highway. Walk about 125 yards to a series of steps that climb up a small incline to an intersection with the Mountains-to-Sea Trail. Proceed straight ahead on the Mountains-to-Sea Trail. It descends along a rocky trail down to a scenic vantage point for Skinny Dip Falls. The path descends to a footbridge near the base of the waterfall. Skinny Dip's several small cascades are accentuated by beautiful clear plunge pools. Skinny Dip Falls is perhaps more of a local hangout than a tourist destination so keep this in mind. It's a great place to swim and wade but the water never gets any warmer than *frigid*. The waterfall descends in a series of three distinct cascades and is much prettier than it appears in any of the photographs I've seen, including my own.

Skinny Dip Falls

Lower Falls ★

Stream: Yellowstone Prong of the
 East Fork Pigeon River
Rating: excellent
Type: steep cascade
Height: 50 feet
Stream flow: small

USGS Quad: Shining Rock, NC
Landowner: Blue Ridge Parkway
Trail length: 0.3 mile (one way)
 or roadside view
Difficulty: moderate
Elevation: 4,960 feet

Directions to the trailhead

From the intersection of U.S. 276 and the Blue Ridge Parkway follow
the parkway south to the Graveyard Fields Overlook (mp 418.8) on the left.

Background

Graveyard Fields is one of the most interesting areas in the southern
Appalachian region. This broad gentle valley is predominantly free of the thick
forest canopy so prominent in the rest of the area. As a result of heavy logging
in the early 1900s, fierce storms which uprooted thousands of trees, and a
spectacular forest fire in 1925 which destroyed over 25,000 acres of dense
forest, the area is surprisingly open and conveys a mystical air about it. The
name is said to have originated from descriptions of the area after thousands of
trees were uprooted; some said the wasteland of stumps and fallen logs looked
like a graveyard.

Twenty-first century visitors can easily explore the area around the
scenic Yellowstone Prong of the East Pigeon River as it meanders through
the gentle valley. The popular Graveyard Fields Trail handles much of the
throng of visitors that come here during the warm weather months when the
Parkway is open. When you see the coloration of the native rock here you will
understand where the stream got its name.

Trail description

To view the falls up close take the trail from the lower end of the
parking area and descend to a footbridge over the Yellowstone Prong at mile
0.15. Cross the footbridge and follow the right fork for approximately 130
yards to a trail fork. Veer right, then turn left immediately and descend a series
of steps and boardwalks down to a point near the base of the falls. (When
in doubt follow the signs). Walk out onto the rocks for the best view of the
waterfall. The cascade features a beautiful boulder-lined plunge pool.

A long range view of the waterfall can be seen from the Blue Ridge
Parkway just a short distance north of the Graveyard Fields Overlook. Yet
another waterfall, Yellowstone Falls, is downstream from Lower Falls but you

cannot see anything from this vantage point and the dangers are just too great. There is no trail to the base. If you absolutely have to get a glimpse of Yellowstone Falls, drive north to milepoint 418.1 on the parkway, about 0.7 mile north of the Graveyard Fields Overlook. From here you see just a small portion of the lower cascades.

*the base and plunge
pool at Lower Falls*

Upper Falls

Stream: Yellowstone Prong of the
    East Fork Pigeon River
Rating: excellent
Type: steep sliding cascade
Height: 40 feet
Stream flow: small

USGS Quad: Shining Rock, NC
Landowner: Blue Ridge Parkway
Trail length: 1.5 miles (one way)
Difficulty: moderate
Elevation: 5,320 feet

Directions to the trailhead
    See directions to Lower Falls on the adjacent page.

Trail description
    From the lower end of the parking lot descend to the footbridge over the Yellowstone Prong at mile 0.15. Turn left and follow the heavily used path for 0.2 mile through an open meadow up to a junction with the Graveyard Fields Connector Trail. Continue straight ahead at this junction following the Yellowstone Prong upstream. About 0.6 mile above the trailhead footbridge

you will come to a fork. Proceed to the right to continue to the waterfall. (On the return trip you can make this an enjoyable loop hike by taking the other fork back to the parking area.) Continue along the trail to the 1.3 mile point where the trail forks at a rock pile. A prominent path goes left but the easiest way to the waterfall is to climb the rocks on the right side of the fork and proceed another 75 yards to the base of the high narrow cascade.

While it's not a *great* waterfall, it is nonetheless quite rugged and the scenery at Graveyard Fields is reason enough to take this hike. If you love the mountains you must pay a visit to this unique location at some point. Recent improvements have helped a great deal. Always follow signage if present.

Wildcat Falls

Stream: tributary of West Fork
    Pigeon River
Rating: excellent
Type: steep sliding cascade
Height: 60 feet
Stream flow: small

USGS Quad: Sam Knob, NC
Landowner: Pisgah National Forest
Trail length: 0.7 mile (one way)
Difficulty: easy
Elevation: 5,200 feet

Directions to the trailhead
    From the intersection of the Blue Ridge Parkway and NC 215 drive north on NC 215 for 0.8 mile. Turn right onto a gravel drive that drops to a small parking area. The drive is a bit steep and might present problems if it has been rainy.

Trail description
    From the parking area at the end of the drive follow the Flat Laurel Creek Trail on an old logging road downhill to Bubbling Springs Branch. Rock hop across the creek then continue along the trail all the way to the cascade at mile 0.7. It's really an easy hike and the only real obstacle is trying to stay dry as you rock hop across the creek. Another smaller creek also has to be crossed but it shouldn't present too much of a problem.

Wildcat Falls

The path roughly parallels the highway and it remains in sight for approximately one-half mile. Beyond that you feel like you're deep in the wilderness. Your arrival at the waterfall is confirmed when you see a large concrete bridge which spans the creek below the upper waterslide. Nearly every visitor I've seen here walks out onto the smooth rock shelf at the base of the high cascade. Be careful as the rocks are very slippery.

Cascades on Bubbling Spring Branch ★

Stream: Bubbling Spring Branch
Rating: excellent
Type: sliding cascade
Height: 75 feet
Stream flow: small

USGS Quad: Sam Knob, NC
Landowner: Pisgah National Forest
Trail length: roadside or short scramble
Difficulty: n/a
Elevation: 4,880 feet

Directions to the trailhead
From the intersection of Blue Ridge Parkway and NC 215 proceed north on NC 215 for 1.9 miles. Turn into the pull-off on the right and park here. Note: there are several pull-offs along the highway in this area. It's one of the last pull-offs as you head down the hill and the cascade is prominently visible from the correct pull-off.

*cascades on
Bubbling Spring Branch*

Description
Don't *ever* pass up a chance to see a good roadside waterfall, and this is one of the best. Also known as "the potholes," the cascades on Bubbling Springs Branch can be viewed from the roadside; you can get an even better view by descending along a rugged path several hundred feet to the base where summertime visitors wade and swim. Another pool is located near the top of the waterfall below a small set of cascades. Definitely check this one out if you're in the area.

Cascades on Sam Branch and Wash Hollow

Stream: Sam Branch   USGS Quad: Sam Knob, NC
Rating: excellent   Landowner: Pisgah National Forest
Type: sliding cascade   Trail length: 0.25 mile (one way)
Height: approx. 100 feet   Difficulty: easy to moderate
Stream flow: small   Elevation: 4,320 feet

Directions to the trailhead

From the intersection of Blue Ridge Parkway and NC 215 proceed north on NC 215 for 4 miles. Look for the curve where the road makes a tight 180-degree left turn. Park along the road shoulder here well off the road.

Trail description

Short and easy is always a good combination, especially when it comes to waterfalls. From the highway pull-off in the curve look for the prominent path that climbs the steep bank up to an old logging road. Turn left and follow the roadbed 0.25 mile to this very scenic set of shallow slides and cascades. The trail actually crosses the creek near the midpoint of the cascade. Unless you want to wade, view the falls from the approach side of the creek.

If the creek is low and you can *safely get across*, continue a few hundred yards along the path to a waterfall in Wash Hollow, a tributary of Sam Branch. This 50-foot cascade features a steep sliding tumble into a small pool.

*scenic cascades
on Sam Branch*

Falls on West Fork Pigeon River

Stream: West Fork Pigeon River
Rating: excellent
Type: long series of cascades
Height: 15 foot main drop
Stream flow: medium

USGS Quad: Sam Knob, NC
Landowner: Pisgah National Forest
Trail length: roadside
Difficulty: n/a
Elevation: 4,160 feet

Directions to the trailhead

From the intersection of Blue Ridge Parkway and NC 215 proceed north on NC 215 for 4.2 miles to the bridge that crosses the West Fork Pigeon River. A small pull-off is located just beyond the bridge on the left. This point is approximately 13.6 miles south of the U.S. 276 and NC 215 intersection.

Description

If you enjoy the raw energy of moving water in a rugged and wild setting this is a good spot to stop as the West Fork Pigeon River roars through a constricted channel over a continuous series of small falls and splashing cascades. A magnificent stone arch bridge soars above one set of powerful cascades. Built by the Civilian Conservation Corps in 1937 this impressive structure is obviously from a time when builders knew how to design aesthetically pleasing structures that were built to last. The bridge is known locally as the "High Arch Bridge." This is a great spot to visit at any season but when the river is high it is a dramatic sight to see.

There is not really one great cascade to single out. As you look upstream among the massive boulders and slabs strewn across the ravine you become aware of the dramatic vertical drop along this portion of the West Fork Pigeon River. Do be careful here. Though inviting, it's really not safe to venture too far out onto these rocks. Some of the slabs slope at ridiculously dangerous angles toward the churning river. They are inviting but quite dangerous.

North Carolina Hub #4 - DuPont State Forest

Normally I might have included these waterfalls in the Rosman and Brevard grouping, but there is so much scenery here that an entire day could easily be spent exploring this remarkable area. The magnificent DuPont State Forest contains over 10,000 acres of spectacular forests and a collection of several of the most impressive waterfalls in the southern Appalachians. If you get a chance research the story behind the founding of this wonderful area. Of particular interest is the battle which culminated in the state of North Carolina invoking eminent domain to acquire the property and save it from a landowner who wished to subdivide the property into an upscale residential development.

Whatever your position on eminent domain happens to be, the result of this battle can now be enjoyed by hikers, horse enthusiasts, mountain bikers,

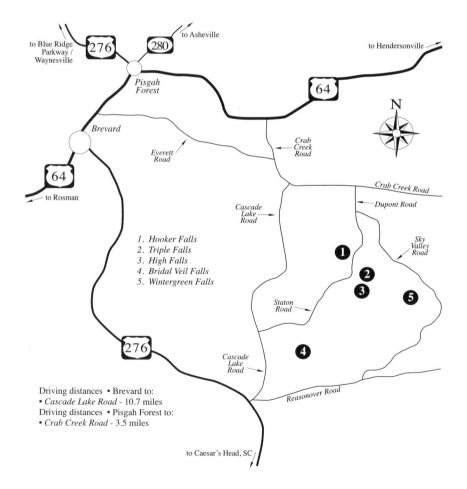

anglers and hunters. Hollywood discovered these waterfalls in the mid-1990s and the film *The Last of the Mohicans* prominently features several of these cascades.

Nearly 100 named trails explore the property and several covered picnic shelters are scattered about as well. Trail descriptions given in this section are generally the shortest or most direct route to the waterfall but numerous trails can be utilized to reach each destination. To maximize your visit guests are highly encouraged to obtain a detailed map of the DuPont State Forest before your visit. Several of DuPont's falls are accessible to persons with disabilities. Go to www.DuPontforest.com for more information or call 828-877-6527.

Hooker Falls ★

Stream: Little River	USGS Quad: Sandingstone Mountain, NC, SC
Rating: excellent	Landowner: DuPont State Forest
Type: free-fall	Trail length: 0.3 mile (one way)
Height: 15 feet	Difficulty: easy
Stream flow: large	Elevation: 2,200 feet

Directions to the trailhead

From the intersection of U.S. 64, U.S. 276 and NC 280 east of downtown Brevard in Pisgah Forest take U.S. 64 east for 3.5 miles. Turn onto Crab Creek Road (#1528). Proceed 4.2 miles and turn right onto DuPont Road (#1259); note: DuPont Road turns into Staton Road when it crosses the Transylvania County line. Drive 3.1 miles to the parking area on the right immediately preceding the Little River bridge.

Trail description

Proceed to the lower right corner of the parking area and follow the gravel road downstream. Keep left along the river and follow the road for 0.3 mile to an overlook at the top of the 15-foot river-wide ledge. Continue along the road to access the base of the waterfall.

Description

Hooker Falls was named for an early settler, Edmund Hooker, who operated a mill at this site in the late 1800s. Hooker certainly was no dummy as the thousands of gallons of water flowing over the waterfall each minute made it a perfect site for a mill. Though the waterfall is only about 15 feet high it is extremely powerful and extends across the entire river channel. Because the waterfall is so close to the parking area nearly anyone can come and take a look. Hooker Falls gets extremely crowded in the warm summer months as it attracts not only waterfall watchers but swimmers, sunbathers and fishing enthusiasts as well. If you want the falls to yourself better get here early.

Hooker Falls

Triple Falls ★

Stream: Little River
Rating: spectacular
Type: three-tiered cascade
Height: 100 feet total
Stream flow: large

USGS Quad: Sandingstone Mountain, NC, SC
Landowner: DuPont State Forest
Trail length: 0.35 mile (one way)
Difficulty: moderate
Elevation: 2,360 feet

Directions to the trailhead
    See directions to Hooker Falls on previous page.

Trail description
    From the trailhead walk to the lower left corner of the parking area, ascend the steps, then turn right and walk to the opposite side of the far end of the bridge. Step over the guard rail and descend to the trail. At the bottom of the steps turn left, then take a quick right at the intersection and begin walking upstream. At mile 0.25 you will reach a fork. Take the right fork and climb to a scenic overlook of Triple Falls. Continue past the overlook to a series of about 90 steps that descend to the rocks along the river near the mid-point of the waterfall. This is a fascinating vantage point to view the middle and upper cascades, but follow the posted guidelines and use good common sense. This is a potentially dangerous area with steep drop-offs and dangerous currents.

Description

      The Little River tumbles over three distinct drops in quick succession to create, in my opinion, one of the most dramatic scenes in the region. The first two drops are about 25 feet high each. The river then makes a quick 90 degree turn to the right and tumbles over a third cascade about 45 feet high. From the upper overlook the three appear one on top of the other, slightly offset to the right. The bare rock around the falls attracts large numbers of sunbathers and provides an ideal viewing platform to enjoy each cascade up close.

Triple Falls

High Falls ★

Stream: Little River	USGS Quad: Sandingstone Mountain, NC, SC
Rating: spectacular	Landowner: DuPont State Forest
Type: steep cascade	Trail length: 1 mile (one way)
Height: 100 feet total	Difficulty: moderate
Stream flow: large	Elevation: 2,480 feet

Directions to the trailhead

      See directions to Hooker Falls on previous page or visitors may also drive to the Buck Forest access area for a shorter route to the falls.

Trail description

      Follow the directions on the previous page to Triple Falls. Continue along the trail past the upper overlook to the trail junction. Turn left and proceed 120 yards to a road fork. Take the left fork onto the High Falls Trail. Proceed down to the river and 0.3 mile to another fork. The right fork climbs along the High Falls Trail for about 300 yards to a series of upper overlooks while the left fork follows the Riverbend Trail along the river to the base.

Description

One of the early names for this waterfall is perhaps the best: *Great Falls*. This magnificent waterfall reminds me of Rainbow Falls on the Horsepasture River - tall, steep and lots of water. What could be one of the most sublime wilderness experiences has been marred somewhat however. A covered bridge is located near the brink and juts out into the scene. It's not terrible but it tends to detract from the "wildness" of the scene. Try your best to ignore this intrusion.

Most of High Fall's flow pushes against the right bank but at high water levels much of the left side of the cliff is covered as well. One of the best views of this cascade is from river level. Locate the prominent side path near the upper overlook that descends to the base. Another route is to veer onto the Riverbend Trail before you reach High Falls. Follow this path several hundred yards up to the base. Both routes give you a fantastic perspective of High Falls.

High Falls

Bridal Veil Falls ★

Stream: Little River
Rating: spectacular
Type: free-fall and slide
Height: 125 feet total
Stream flow: medium

USGS Quad: Sandingstone Mountain, NC,SC
Landowner: DuPont State Forest
Trail length: 2 miles (one way)
Difficulty: moderate
Elevation:2,640 feet

Directions to the trailhead

From downtown Brevard take U.S. 276 south for 10.7 miles. Turn left onto Cascade Lake Road. Proceed several hundred yards then turn right onto

Reasonover Road. Proceed 2.7 miles to Fawn Lake access are on the left.

If you are coming from the Hooker Falls access area, go south on Staton Road for 2.3 miles. Turn left onto Cascade Lake Road and proceed 2.4 miles to Reasonover Road then drive 2.7 miles to Fawn Lake access area.

Trail description

From the Fawn Lake access area take the Reasonover Creek Trail northeast. Turn left onto Conservation Road in about 200 yards and start walking. In 0.8 mile cross an old airstrip; stay on Conservation Road and descend past several houses and a maintenance shed. Several hundred yards after passing Julia Lake Road on the right look for Bridal Veil Road on the left at mile 1.5. Follow Bridal Veil Road for 0.5 mile to the base of the falls.

Description

This massive waterfall is a challenge to accurately describe. It is dramatically different from nearly every other waterfall in this guide. It begins by free-falling over an overhanging ledge then sliding 200 yards over a sloping dome of exposed bedrock. The river fans out gracefully and covers most of the dome in a magnificent veil (hence the name) as it completes its descent. Descriptions are tough; come see it for yourself.

Be sure to read the park's list of do's and don'ts, especially as they pertain to the park's waterfalls. Most of the waterfalls in the DuPont Forest have a great deal of exposed rock around them so you don't have to contend with underbrush to get really close. Bridal Veil is no exception as a path leads up the left side of the dome taking hikers to the top of the upper cascades.

the base of Bridal Veil Falls

Wintergreen Falls

Stream: Grassy Creek
Rating: excellent
Type: cascade and free-fall
Height: 20 feet total
Stream flow: medium

USGS Quad: Sandingstone Mountain, NC, SC
Landowner: DuPont State Forest
Trail length: 1.3 miles (one way)
Difficulty: moderate
Elevation: 2,600 feet

Directions to the trailhead

From the intersection of U.S. 64, U.S. 276 and NC 280 east of downtown Brevard (Pisgah Forest area) take U.S. 64 east for 3.5 miles and turn onto Crab Creek Road (#1528). Proceed 4.2 miles and turn right onto DuPont Road (#1259). Proceed 0.7 mile and turn left onto Sky Valley Road (#1260) and drive 1.5 miles to Guion Farm access area on the right.

Trail description

Proceed to the south end of the parking area to the information board. Walk across the field and into the woods on the Tarkiln Branch Trail. Proceed to a fork and go right. Walk to just beyond the 1 mile point and come to yet another fork. The trail to Wintergreen Falls goes left. Continue along the path to the creek. A prominent path drops about 75 yards down to the base of the falls.

Though it isn't in the same league as the previous DuPont waterfalls described on the previous pages, Wintergreen is still a very scenic destination and perfect if you're looking for smaller crowds. The cascade has a beautiful plunge pool that may prove tempting in the hot summer months. Most of the crowds will flock to the larger falls so with a bit of luck you may have Wintergreen all to yourself.

Other Notable North Carolina Waterfalls

It's very difficult knowing where to close this publication when so many other notable waterfalls are out there waiting. My personal goal is to continue to add waterfall hubs with each printing for as long as I am able to do so. In the meantime, there are four additional waterfalls of note that I would like to include - two on the Blue Ridge Parkway north and east of Asheville, one near the South Carolina line south of Asheville, and one in magnificent Hickory Nut Gorge southeast of Asheville. I plan to expand the waterfall listings in North Carolina and Tennessee in the very near future.

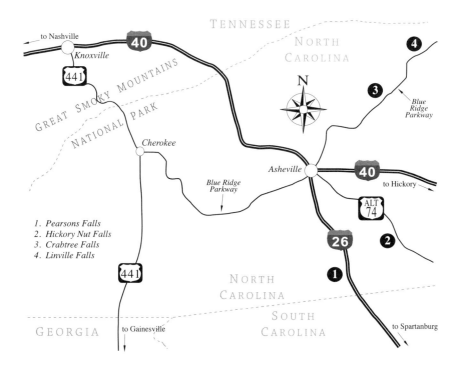

1. Pearsons Falls
2. Hickory Nut Falls
3. Crabtree Falls
4. Linville Falls

Pearson's Falls ★

Stream: Colt Creek
Rating: excellent
Type: multi-tiered cascade
Height: 75 feet
Stream flow: small

USGS Quad: Saluda, NC, SC
Landowner: Tryon Garden Club
Trail length: 0.3 miles (one way)
Difficulty: easy to moderate
Elevation: 1,600 feet

Directions to the trailhead
From I-26 southeast of Saluda take exit 59. Proceed west on Ozone Drive for 1.1 miles. Turn left onto NC 176 and proceed downhill for 2.5 miles to Pearson Falls Road (#1102) on the right. Drive 0.9 mile to the entrance. Currently a fee of $5 per adult and $2 per child (under 6 free) is required to enter and view the waterfall and grounds. Check the Pearson's Falls website for seasonal hours of operation.

Background and description
The Tryon Garden Club purchased this wonderful area in 1931 and has managed it since that time. The waterfall was discovered by Charles William Pearson in the years after the Civil War while scouting possible routes for the Southern Railroad from Spartanburg, South Carolina, to Asheville, North Carolina (as a sidenote this line is notable in railroad circles as one of the steepest grades in operation in North America).

This beautiful 75-foot cascade tumbles over a stairstepping series of small ledges into the peaceful glen. The area is botanically rich with over 200 species of native plants; the glen is particularly renowned for its wonderful

display of seasonal wildflowers. The Tryon Garden Club has published a booklet *Pearson's Falls Glen* that provides additional details about this remarkable site. Go to www.pearsonsfalls.org for more information.

Pearson's Falls

Hickory Nut Falls ★

Stream: Fall Creek
Rating: excellent
Type:steep waterslide/cascade
Height: 350+ feet
Stream flow: small

USGS Quad: Bat Cave, NC
Landowner: Chimney Rock Park
Trail length: 0.7 to base (one way)
    or 1.5 miles for complete loop
Difficulty: easy to base/ strenuous for loop
Elevation: 2,440 feet

Directions to the trail head
  Chimney Rock Park is located on U.S. 64/U.S. 74 Alt in Hickory Nut Gorge in the busy tourist hamlet of Chimney Rock. Turn onto the park entrance road and drive up the mountain to the admission booth. An entrance fee is required. Proceed to the large parking lot further up the mountain.

Description
  Dramatic Chimney Rock rises high above spectacular Hickory Nut Gorge near incomparable Lake Lure. You can hardly miss the world famous landmark as an enormous American flag flies high above the rocky buttress. Likewise it's hard to miss Hickory Nut Falls, even from the highway, as it tumbles several hundred feet down a smooth sheer cliff into the rocky gorge.
  The waterfall gained tremendous notoriety due to its presence in several scenes from the 1992 film *The Last of the Mohicans*. The film's epic climactic chase and fight scenes were filmed at the brink of the spectacular waterfall.
  Interestingly, the park claims the height of the waterfall at 404', yet several other independent authorities claim somewhat less. One unofficial measurement from the brink to the plunge pool came in at 351 feet. Either way it is undoubtedly beautiful, particularly during periods of high water flow. In the late summer and fall the cascade diminishes greatly unless you happen to be fortunate enough to visit after a heavy rainstorm.
  The 0.7 mile walk to the base of the falls is relatively flat and not too difficult, but the 1.5 mile loop hike requires quite a few stairs as you tackle the approximate 400-foot change in elevation. Most people find this quite strenuous but the views of Hickory Nut Gorge and Lake Lure from the upper trail are well worth it. You can't see the waterfall from the brink but there are several scenic cascades just upstream of the main drop. As the trail descends and you pass the base of the waterfall there are some good photo opportunities of the lower portion of the cascade, though it's nearly impossible to get the entire cascade in one shot. Try zooming in to isolate one particular section and you may come away with a nice remembrance of the falls.

Crabtree Falls ★

Stream: Big Crabtree Creek	USGS Quad: Celo, NC
Rating: excellent	Landowner: Blue Ridge Parkway
Type: steep cascade	Trail length: 1.0 mile (one way)
Height: 70 feet	Difficulty: moderate
Stream flow: small	Elevation: 3,360 feet

Directions to the trailhead

Crabtree Meadows is located along the Blue Ridge Parkway at mile 339.5, about 8.5 miles south of NC 226 in Little Switzerland and 4.5 miles north of NC 80 at Buck Gap. Crabtree Meadows is approximately 15 miles northwest of Marion, North Carolina. The campground is seasonal and visitors in the early spring may have to park at the gate and walk to the trailhead. For more details obtain a free trail system map at the campground check-in station.

Trail and description

From the trailhead parking area proceed about 250 yards to a trail junction. If you want to take the shortest route to the falls go right. It is 0.85 mile one way with a moderate descent. If you hike the entire loop it is approximately 2.5 miles. The waterfall is named for the old crabapple orchards found on the farms of the area. Several of these orchards were located just upstream of the falls in the decades before the parkway was built.

Crabtree Falls is an impressive 70-foot cascade which spills over a steep cliff with dozens of small striated bumps and ledges. The waterfall fans out across the ledge as it descends. This is a popular stop along the parkway so be ready for crowds in the summer months.

Crabtree Falls

Linville Falls ★

Stream: Linville River
Rating: spectacular
Type: large cascade
Height: 50 feet
Stream flow: large

USGS Quad: Linville Falls, NC
Landowner: Blue Ridge Parkway
Trail length: approx. 1.0 mile (one way)
Difficulty: moderate
Elevation: 3,120 feet

Directions to the trailhead

The Linville Falls visitor center is located on the Blue Ridge Parkway at milepost 316.3, about one mile north of the U.S. 221 intersection. The falls are located between the towns of Linville Falls and Linville.

History

Rugged Linville Falls was known as *The Great Falls* to the Cherokee who made this area their home. The falls are named after William Linville, an early explorer who was killed by the Cherokees while in the area in 1766. This area has a very interesting history that makes for some fascinating reading. Linville Gorge is the deepest gorge in eastern North America and its location along the Blue Ridge Parkway makes it one of the most popular attractions in the region.

Trail and description

At the head of this spectacular gorge Linville Falls punges in several stages over an enormous cliff. From the visitor center just off the parkway several excellent trails lead to a number of outstanding overlooks with colorful names such as Erwin's View, Chimney View and Plunge Basin. Detailed maps are posted at the visitor center. Take your time and view these wonderful waterfalls from several overlooks. Generally the trails that go downstream on the right side of the river lead to overlooks high above the river while the trails to the left feature an upper overlook and a trail that descends to the base.

Linville Falls

Section IV

The Great
Smoky Mountains
National Park

The Great Smoky Mountains National Park

The Great Smoky Mountains National Park is America's most heavily visited national park. Around ten million visitors each year enter the 520,000-acre park which contains sixteen peaks exceeding 6,000 feet in elevation. The park is rich in Cherokee and pioneer history and locations like Cades Cove, Cataloochee and Oconaluftee are treasure troves of this region's rich history. Over 800 miles of hiking trails provide access to every corner of this spectacular park, and many of these trails lead to lovely waterfalls. The park really isn't known as a haven for big waterfalls but those that are found here are quite enchanting.

While the park's visitation numbers are staggering, the vast majority of visitors never venture far from the north/south Highway 441 corridor as they drive from Cherokee to Gatlinburg. There are two major visitor centers at each gateway town - the Oconaluftee Visitors Center is located on the southern end of the park near Cherokee, while the Sugarlands visitor center is just outside Gatlinburg. Both visitor centers have excellent gift shops operated by the Great Smoky Mountains Association where visitors may obtain additional information via an extensive collection of books and maps detailing the park.

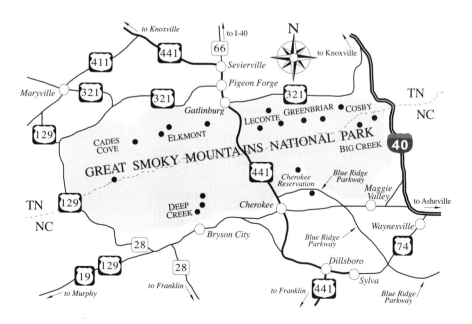

Waterfalls in the Elkmont Section of the Park

Laurel Falls ★

Stream: Laurel Branch

Rating: excellent

Type: cascade

Height: 80 feet

Stream flow: medium

USGS Quad: Gatlinburg, TN

Landowner: GSMNP - Elkmont section

Trail length: 1.3 miles (one way)

Difficulty: easy to moderate

Elevation: 2,680 feet

Directions to the trailhead

From the Sugarlands Visitor Center on U.S. 441 just outside of Gatlinburg turn onto Little River Road (Hwy. 73) and proceed 3.8 miles to the Laurel Falls Trail on the right located in Fighting Creek Gap.

Trail and description

An interpretive brochure is available at the trailhead for a small fee. Laurel Falls is a wonderful 80-foot cascade that is one of the most heavily visited waterfalls in the park. Its location near the gateway town of Gatlinburg has a lot to do with this. So many visitors want to see Laurel Falls that the entire 1.3 mile trail is paved. Heavy crowds may impact your visit but at least trail conditions are pretty consistent.

One of the more unusual aspects of Laurel Falls is the way the trail bisects the cascade near its midpoint. The path then rock-hops across the stream to the opposite bank. On the far side you have a really nice vantage point from which to view and enjoy the cascade. The falls are beautifully framed between banks of lush rhododendron, and the area around the waterfall is in really good shape considering the amount of human traffic.

upper cascades
Laurel Falls

The Sinks ★

Stream: Little River
Rating: excellent
Type: cascade
Height: 15 feet
Stream flow: large

USGS Quad: Wear Cove, TN
Landowner: GSMNP - Elkmont section
Trail length: roadside
Difficulty: n/a
Elevation: 1,560 feet

Directions to the trailhead

From the Sugarlands Visitor Center on U.S. 441 just outside of Gatlinburg turn onto Little River Road (Hwy. 73) and proceed 12 miles to the bridge over the river at the Sinks. Turn left into the parking area. This Sinks is located 6 miles east of the Townsend entrance to the park.

Description

The Sinks is a large natural swimming hole formed as the river quiets just below a powerful 10-foot drop on the Little River. Entire generations have come to swim in the huge pool and jump from the rocky ledge above it. The Little River has outgrown its name by the time it gets to the Sinks and though the ledge isn't too impressive on its own the amount of water that surges over the ledge creates a very scenic setting. While I cannot recommend or condone jumping from cliffs into the river, you can witness it here on nearly any given summer day. The National Park Service has posted a warning here as to the dangers of The Sinks. Even if you don't dip a toe in the water it's a great place to stop and watch the show.

The Sinks

Miegs Falls ★

Stream: Miegs Creek
Rating: excellent
Type: steep cascade
Height: 30 feet
Stream flow: medium

USGS Quad: Wear Cove, TN
Landowner: GSMNP - Elkmont section
Trail length: roadside
Difficulty: n/a
Elevation: approx. 1,440 feet

Directions to the trailhead

From the Sugarlands Visitor Center on U.S. 441 just outside of Gatlinburg turn onto Little River Road (Hwy. 73) and proceed 13 miles to an extended paved pull-off on the left side of the road. This pull-off is located 5 miles east of the Townsend entrance to the park.

Description

The Little River Road and its never ending parade of scenery is one of the prettiest drives in the entire park. Waterfall lovers in particular will enjoy the dozens of scenic shoals and small cascades along the river. This particular stretch is a bit more scenic than others as beautiful Miegs Falls adds to the scenery. Miegs tumbles over a steep 30-foot ledge before making a quick 125 yard dash to the surging Little River. The view of the falls looks across the river and into a shallow cove. It would be great if the park would construct a footbridge that would allow visitors to walk back to the cascade, but don't hold your breath. The view from the highway is unobstructed in the winter but portions of the cascade can be obscured during the warm weather months.

telephoto lens shot of Miegs Falls

Waterfalls in the LeConte Section of the Park

Rainbow Falls ★

Stream: LeConte Creek
Rating: excellent
Type: free-fall
Height: 75 feet
Stream flow: small

USGS Quad: Mt. LeConte, TN, NC
Landowner: GSMNP - LeConte section
Trail length: 2.7 miles (one way)
Difficulty: strenuous (elevation gain)
Elevation: 4,300 feet

Directions to the trailhead
    In downtown Gatlinburg proceed to traffic signal #8 and turn onto Airport Road. Drive one mile and enter the Great Smoky Mountains National Park. The name of the road changes here to Cherokee Orchard Road. Proceed 2.5 miles to the Rainbow Falls parking area.

Trail and description
    This 75-foot beauty is one of the best waterfalls in the Smokies, but with a near 1,700 foot change in elevation you'll definitely earn your view. In a rare free-fall from a sheer sandstone cliff, Rainbow Falls does indeed offer up a rainbow if water flow and light conditions are just right. The downside is that because the waterfall is located high in the LeConte Creek watershed the stream is somewhat small; if it has been dry this waterfall can virtually disappear. For waterfall watchers this is not a good thing, especially after 2.7 miles of uphill hiking. If you plan your visit when the creek is high it's an entirely different story. During wet periods the waterfall features a large spray zone as the free-falling water pounds the rocks at the base.
    The climb is along a consistent but moderate uphill grade. Don't kill yourself heading uphill - the trail provides plenty of good spots to sit and rest. Only the most determined hikers will want to continue beyond the waterfall to the top of lofty Mt. LeConte. It's an additional 4 miles to the top and the total change in elevation is about 4,000 feet making it one of the most challenging trails in the Smokies.
    As fate would have it, every time I have had the opportunity to visit Rainbow Falls the creek has been low. While it's always a great hike and the falls are interesting no matter how much water is in LeConte Creek, this one is at the top of my list to visit when it's at its best. The trail and waterfall receive heavy use. Plan your trip accordingly.

Grotto Falls ★

Stream: Roaring Fork
Rating: excellent
Type: cascade
Height: 20 feet
Stream flow: medium

USGS Quad: Mt. LeConte, TN, NC
Landowner: GSMNP - LeConte section
Trail length: 1.5 miles (one way)
Difficulty: moderate (steady uphill climb)
Elevation: 3,720 feet

Directions to the trailhead

In downtown Gatlinburg proceed to traffic signal #8 and turn onto Airport Road. Drive 1 mile and enter the Great Smoky Mountains National Park. The name of the road changes to Cherokee Orchard Road. Proceed 2.8 miles and turn onto the Roaring Fork Auto Trail. Proceed 2 miles to the Grotto Falls Trail on the right. *Note:* pray for a parking space and hope for a miracle. *Note #2*: Don't plan a winter visit; the auto trail is closed in the winter months.

Trail and description

Obtain a copy of the *Roaring Fork Auto Trail* at the gate for a small fee. This booklet will provide a great deal of history about this historic area. Before you visit be aware that this is a very popular hike and you will probably be in the company of hundreds of people during the peak season. If you like solitude or smaller crowds be sure to come early. The auto trail is quite busy as well. It doesn't pay to be in a hurry when visiting here.

Grotto Falls is a scenic 20-foot drop that occurs along the Roaring Fork, one of the all-time great stream names in the Smokies (someone should open a restaurant at the edge of the park and call it *The Roaring Fork*). The waterfall plunges from the flanks of a steep overhanging rock ledge into a broad but shallow plunge pool. Visitors follow the trail behind the thin veil of falling water through a deep recess in the ledge. Several good cascades occur both upstream and downstream of Grotto Falls so there's more to see besides the waterfall. Grotto Falls is located about half-way along the magnificent hike to Trillium Gap so there are plenty of opportunities for enjoyable day hikes in this part of the park.

Grotto Falls

Place-of-a-Thousand-Drips

Stream: Cliff Branch
Rating: excellent
Type: free-fall
Height: 20 feet
Stream flow: medium

USGS Quad: Mt. LeConte, TN, NC
Landowner: GSMNP - LeConte section
Trail length: roadside
Difficulty: n/a
Elevation: approx. 1,800 feet

Directions to the trailhead
Follow the directions on the previous page to the Grotto Falls Trail parking area. From here continue an additional 2.9 miles to a pull-off on the right. Note: the auto trail is closed in the winter months.

Description
This name is about as accurate as any when it comes to describing this unusual cascade that tumbles, surges, drops, fizzles, and yes, drips alongside the busy Roaring Fork Auto Trail. The-Place-of-a-Thousand-Drips could also be called Swiss Cheese Falls due to the dozens of routes the creek follows as it tumbles down a steep rock wall covered with mosses and lichens. Cliff Branch tumbles a few feet, disappears, then resurfaces a few yards away before rushing off in yet another direction. There are quite a few photos in various publications showing this cascade and in my opinion none of them does it justice, including all that I have taken here over the years. The rock wall is so massive that the tiny cascades nearly disappear in images of the entire waterfall. The best way to capture The-Place-of-a-Thousand-Drips in a photograph may be to isolate just a small portion of the cascade (but then you lose the overall effect).

The total drop over this sandstone ledge is around 75 feet. Across the road the scenic Roaring Fork continues its frenzied descent toward Gatlinburg. Waterfall saavy visitors may have noticed another small cascade several hundred yards back up the road. You can stroll back to get a closer look but watch for oncoming traffic as the Roaring Fork's traffic flow is usually fairly steady and drivers can be a bit preoccupied with the scenery.

Waterfalls in the Greenbrier Section of the Park

Fern Branch Falls

Stream: Fern Branch
Rating: good
Type: cascade/waterslide
Height: 50 feet
Stream flow: small

USGS Quad: Mt. LeConte, TN, NC
Landowner: GSMNP - Greenbrier section
Trail length: 1.8 miles (one way)
Difficulty: moderate
Elevation: approx. 2,300 feet

Directions to the trailhead

In downtown Gatlinburg turn onto Hwy. 321 east and drive 6 miles. Turn right into the Greenbrier section of the park and proceed 4 miles to the Porters Creek trailhead.

Trail and description

The Greenbrier section of the park is a bit off the beaten path and doesn't get the crushing visitation that the central corridor attracts. Because of this many of its scenic attractions can be enjoyed without the elbow-to-elbow experiences so common at waterfalls such as Laurel Falls near Gatlinburg. A pretty 1.8 mile (one way) stroll along scenic Porters Creek leads hikers to a small but pretty cascade that rushes over a steep rock wall into a beautiful green cove blanketed with mosses, ferns and seasonal wildflowers. In fact, this trail is known as one of the best spring wildflower hikes in the Smokies.

The trail follows an old roadbed for one mile up into the Porters Creek watershed passing the Smoky Mountain Hiking Club cabin and a number of pretty shoals along the route. A log footbridge crosses the creek at mile 1.5; proceed 0.3 mile further and you'll arrive at the waterfall. This is one of my favorite Smokies scenes as nearly every exposed rock along the creek is covered with a lush green growth of native mosses. As the name implies, ferns abound near the waterfall. In the spring and summer it offers a scene of overwhelming greenery. Visit during the peak of fall color and the contrasts between the leaves and the moss covered rocks can be striking. Be sure to keep your eyes open for evidence of early settlers as you hike the trail.

Ramsey Cascades ★

Stream: Ramsey Prong	USGS Quad: Mt. Guyot, TN, NC
Rating: excellent	Landowner: GSMNP - Greenbrier section
Type: cascade	Trail length: 4 miles (one way)
Height: 100 feet	Difficulty: strenuous (2,000' elevation gain)
Stream flow: medium	Elevation: 4,300 feet

Directions to the trailhead

In downtown Gatlinburg turn onto Hwy. 321 east and drive 6 miles. Turn right into the Greenbrier section of the park and proceed 3.2 miles to the bridge on the left. Turn here onto Ramsey Prong Road and drive alongside the splashing river for 1.5 miles to the dead end. Park here.

Trail and description

To put it bluntly, this is one of the most strenuous hikes in this book; if you're looking for something easy - this ain't it. At 100 feet, Ramsey Cascades is the tallest waterfall in the park and without doubt one of the best. It plunges over a steep cliff face between boulders and fractured rocks dropping over nine stair-stepping ledges to a trail crossing just below the waterfall. If eight miles of hiking isn't enough to dissuade you visiting, perhaps the 2000-foot elevation gain will. You'd better be in really good shape or you'll turn back from exhaustion before ever reaching the waterfall.

The initial 1.5 miles of the Ramsey Cascades Trail treads an old road that passes through scenic boulder fields and beautiful old-growth forests. The trail rarely strays far from the noisy Ramsey Prong. Numerous stream crossings are required so be prepared to get your feet a bit wet.

The final 2.5 miles is along a heavily used trail that can get quite muddy when the weather is wet. This portion of the trail is also much steeper and the grade rarely lets up as you climb high into the watershed. Hikers wind through a maze of huge boulders as the trail approaches the waterfall. The setting is wild and truly beautiful. If you're hungry for more, the trail continues about 0.5 mile further to a beautiful series of pools known as Drinkwater Pool, and yet another nice waterfall is 0.5 mile beyond.

Use good common sense when visiting Ramsey Cascades. There have been dozens of injuries and several fatalities. This waterfall is a long way from civilization and help would be a long time coming. *Stay off the waterfall and stay away from the top of the cascade.*

Waterfalls in the Cades Cove Section of the Park

Abrams Falls ★

Stream: Abrams Creek
Rating: excellent
Type: steep cascade
Height: 25 feet
Stream flow: large

USGS Quad: Calderwood, TN, NC
Landowner: GSMNP - Cades Cove section
Trail length: 2.5 miles (one way)
Difficulty: moderate
Elevation: approx. 1,490 feet

Directions to the trailhead

From Gatlinburg follow Little River Road west to the Townsend entrance of the park. Turn onto Laurel Creek Road and proceed into Cades Cove. Follow the one-way loop around the cove for 5 miles. Cross the Abrams Creek bridge then turn right and follow the gravel road to the Abrams Falls trailhead.

Trail and description

Abrams Falls is one of the most popular waterfalls in the Great Smoky Mountains National Park and for good reason. This is a prime destination along a beautiful 2.5 mile (one way) hike. All streams in Cades Cove eventually empty into Abrams Creek making it the only large stream in the cove.

The trail follows a wide, rocky roadbed for most of its length. Stony Ridge and Arbutus Ridge offer minor grades as you make your way toward the waterfall. Neither is particularly challenging but they will get your heart pumping. Arbutus Ridge is noteworthy in that it shortcuts an unusual horseshoe bend in the river. Just before you reach the waterfall the trail crosses Wilson Creek.

This powerful 25-foot cascade tumbles into a massive open plunge pool. When the creek is high, spray fills the air and moistens everything close to the falls. The rocks around the pool are a great spot to picnic, people watch, and catch a few rays. It is a popular attraction and stays crowded in the summer months and on warm weather weekends.

A side trail drops down to the top of the cascade. The brink is a popular stop but

Abrams Falls

is actually quite dangerous. Play it safe and continue to the base where the view is magnificent. Most hikers retrace their steps back to the cove, but other trails intersect downstream offering great hiking possibilities.

Spruce Flats Falls

Stream: Spruce Flats Branch
Rating: good
Type: cascade
Height: 100 feet total
Stream flow: small

USGS Quad: Wear Cove, TN
Landowner: GSMNP - Cades Cove section
Trail length: 1.0 mile (one way)
Difficulty: moderate
Elevation: approx. 1,400 feet

Directions to the trailhead

Starting at the Townsend park entrance proceed west along Laurel Creek Road for 0.2 mile. Turn left onto Tremont Road and proceed 2 miles. Turn left into the Great Smoky Mountains Institute parking area.

Trail and description

Spruce Flats Falls is a pretty multi-tiered cascade that is accessed via an undulating one mile hike that originates at the Great Smoky Mountains Institute. The entire series of cascades drops about 100 feet in total though each cascade is separate and distinct. From the vantage point at the base three of the cascades are visible. Just upstream and slightly out of view is a fourth. It's not a heavily visited cascade but is still a nice destination if time is limited.

From the Great Smoky Mountains Institute parking area follow the road leading to staff housing. Locate the side trail marked "falls." This trail features a few steep grades before moderating for the balance of the hike. It parallels the rushing Middle Prong upstream before dropping to the Spruce Flat Branch just downstream of the cascades.

Spruce Flats Falls

Waterfalls in the Cosby Section

Hen Wallow Falls

Stream: Hen Wallow Creek   USGS Quad: Hartford, TN, NC
Rating: good   Landowner: GSMNP - Cosby section
Type: steep cascade   Trail length: 2.0 miles (one way)
Height: 90 feet   Difficulty: moderate
Stream flow: small   Elevation: 2,000 feet

Directions to the trailhead

From Gatlinburg turn onto Hwy. 321 and drive east for 19 miles to Cosby. Turn right onto Hwy. 32 and proceed 1.5 miles south to the Cosby campground road. Drive 2 miles to the day hikers and picnic area parking lot on the left. Walk to the Gabes Mountain Trail just across the road from the parking entrance.

Trail and description

There's a lot to like about the magnificent serenity of the Smokies' Cosby section. One of Cosby's secrets, Hen Wallow Falls, is found at the end of a moderate 2 mile hike along the scenic Gabes Mountain Trail. It is actually one of the park's tallest cascades but it doesn't receive the crushing visitation of some of the park's other cascades.

From the trailhead proceed along an old roadbed for 0.25 mile. This path connects with a spur trail that comes from the nearby Cosby campground. Continue along the main path and cross Rock Creek over a footbridge. The trail meanders through a beautiful forest setting typical of the Great Smoky Mountains National Park with highlights including pretty displays of wildflowers in the spring and native rhododendrons in the early summer.

Crying Creek is reached at mile 1.1 and just beyond this point the trail merges with the Gabes Mountain Trail which comes in from the right. Continue straight ahead to mile 2.0 where a 200-yard side trail drops to the base of this lovely cascade as it races down a near vertical rock face. The base is littered with jagged boulders and fragmented rocks. Much of the cliff is covered in beautiful mosses and lichens. Visit in the summertime and the contrast between the lush greenery and the black cliff face is striking. Because the stream is small be sure to visit Hen Wallow Falls during periods of ample flow.

Waterfalls in the Big Creek Section

Midnight Hole

Stream: Big Creek   USGS Quad: Luftee Knob, NC, TN
Rating: good   Landowner: GSMNP - Big Creek section
Type: small cascade   Trail length: 1.4 miles (one way)
Height: 8 feet   Difficulty: moderate
Stream flow: large   Elevation: approx. 2,200 feet

Directions to the trailhead

From I-40 on the park's eastern flank take the Waterville exit. Cross the bridge over the Pigeon River then turn south (left). Proceed 2 miles through Waterville then continue approximately 0.8 mile to the picnic area and campground. Note: the road may be gated at the ranger station in the winter.

Trail and description

The creatively named Big Creek is one of the largest and most impressive streams in the park. This large cascading "creek" stays within earshot for much of the length of the scenic Big Creek Trail. This popular path covers nearly 6 miles as it ascends from the campground to Walnut Bottoms.

There are several nice waterfalls that can be viewed from this trail and dozens of other sights as well. Midnight Hole is one of the first attractions. It's not much of a waterfall but it is worth including because its such a scenic destination. Midnight Hole is formed as twin 8-foot "waterfalls" plunge from a large boulder pile into an inviting pool. It's one of the most popular swimming holes in the park but don't expect much in the way of pleasant water conditions. It's icy cold, even in the stifling heat of the summer. The 1.4 mile walk is enough to ward off many would-be visitors but the Midnight Hole

can still become quite crowded at times. As the name suggests it has perhaps been the scene of more than one nocturnal adventure.

Midnight Hole

Mouse Creek Falls

Stream: Mouse Creek   USGS Quad: Luftee Knob, TN, NC
Rating: excellent   Landowner: GSMNP - Big Creek section
Type: cascade   Trail length: 2 miles (one way)
Height: 50 feet   Difficulty: moderate
Stream flow: large   Elevation: 2,320 feet

Directions to the trailhead

Follow the directions on the previous page to Midnight Hole. Continue past Midnight Hole on the Big Creek Trail for an additional 0.6 mile (2 miles from the trailhead).

Trail and description

If Midnight Hole isn't enough to whet your appetite the Big Creek Trail offers up something a bit more traditional in the category of falling water about 0.6 mile ahead. This is Mouse Creek Falls, a steep two-tiered ledge that rushes down a series of lively cascades and right into the surging waters of Big Creek. Streamside boulders and rocks are covered with beautiful mosses and the cascade is framed in a shaded grove of dense rhododendron. The cascade is somewhat reminiscent of an hourglass as it begins wide, narrows at the midpoint then fans out again near the base. A perfectly placed bench provides a great spot to sit and enjoy this scenic cascade.

If you're really looking for a challenge you might consider hiking beyond Mouse Creek Falls all the way up to **Gunter Fork Cascades**. Gunter Fork Cascades features a 25-foot cascading drop followed by a long series of small cascades that drop about 100-feet over the course of a 300-foot run. The additional 6 miles takes a great deal of energy and while the waterfall is nice the scenery throughout this part of the park is really the attraction. Because of the 8.2 mile (one way) trek, many visitors make a reservation with the park to camp in Walnut Bottoms (5.8 mile from the trailhead). Obtain a detailed Great Smoky Mountains map or guide and check out all your options.

Waterfalls in the Deep Creek Section

Juneywhank Falls

Stream: Juneywhank Creek   USGS Quad: Bryson City, NC
Rating: good   Landowner: GSMNP - Deep Creek section
Type: small cascade   Trail length: 0.3 mile (one way)
Height: 50 feet   Difficulty: easy to moderate
Stream flow: small   Elevation: approx. 1,940 feet

Directions to the trailhead

From downtown Bryson City follow the signs to the Deep Creek campground and picnic area. Enter the park boundary and proceed straight ahead for 0.6 mile past the picnic area to the trailhead parking area. One of the paths to the waterfall begins here; another begins just ahead at the beginning of the Deep Creek Trail.

Trail and description

There's a great deal to see and do in the Deep Creek section of the park and Juneywhank Falls probably isn't at the top of the list. However it only takes about 15 minutes to view this small cascade as it descends toward its confluence with Deep Creek. One path to the falls begins at the point where Juneywhank Creek runs under the road. It climbs uphill to the 50-foot cascade which is bisected by a recently constructed footbridge with a bench situated right in front of the waterfall. There are signs in place to help you find the trailheads. Juneywhank is a good primer to the other larger falls that you can visit as you head up the Deep Creek Trail.

Juneywhank Falls

Tom's Branch Falls

Stream: Tom's Branch
Rating: excellent
Type: small cascade
Height: 60 feet
Stream flow: small

USGS Quad: Bryson City, NC
Landowner: GSMNP - Deep Creek section
Trail length: 0.2 mile (one way)
Difficulty: easy
Elevation: approx. 1,880 feet

Directions to the trailhead

From downtown Bryson City follow the signs to the Deep Creek campground and picnic area. Enter the park boundary and proceed straight ahead for 0.6 mile into the picnic area to the parking area at the dead end.

Trail and description

The Deep Creek Trail provides access to two beautiful waterfalls and the first, Tom's Branch Falls, is just 0.2 mile from the trailhead. This delightful trail is sidewalk flat for 0.4 mile up to a large footbridge which spans the rushing creek. It's a popular stretch of the river for tubers and chances are you'll have plenty of company if you visit in the summer months.

Tom's Branch Falls is a small cascade that stairsteps about 60 feet down a steep ravine before plunging directly into Deep Creek. Portions of the drop are visible year round but in the leafless winter months nearly the entire cascade is visible. Some nice photographs can be made by framing the falls with a large tree in the foreground. It's a highly scenic spot if you don't mind sharing it with scores of walkers, hikers, and throngs of tubers. Several nice benches face the creek and waterfall. It's a great place to sit and enjoy the scene, but because of its proximity to the trailhead you'll rarely view it alone.

Tom's Branch Falls

Indian Creek Falls ★

Stream: Indian Creek
Rating: excellent
Type: steep cascade
Height: 25 feet
Stream flow: medium

USGS Quad: Bryson City, NC
Landowner: GSMNP - Deep Creek section
Trail length: 1 mile (one way)
Difficulty: easy
Elevation: approx. 1,900 feet

Directions to the trailhead

See directions on previous page to Tom's Branch Falls.

Trail and description

Waterfall number three accessed via the Deep Creek Trail is the best of the lot. Indian Creek Falls is a nice 25-foot cascade that races down a steep dome of bedrock into a shallow plunge pool set amidst banks of fragrant rhododendron and laurel.

From the trailhead parking area follow the Deep Creek Trail upstream to the large footbridge at mile 0.4. The trail continues along an old roadbed but now heads moderately uphill. A number of nice shoals and cascades are within easy view as you look down the steep creek bank to the left. At mile 0.9 fork right and follow the Indian Creek Trail for about 100 yards up to a side path on the left that scrambles down to the waterfall.

If you'd like to make this walk into a challenging loop hike then continue hiking past the waterfall along the Indian Creek Trail. Pass the Thomas Divide Trail on the right at mile 1.4. At mile point 1.7 a loop trail connector intersects from the left. Take the loop trail and climb about 350 feet over the next half mile to the top of Sunkota Ridge. Descend back to the Deep Creek Trail then turn left and follow the path back to the parking area. This option adds approximately 2 miles to the hike.

Indian Creek Falls

Waterfalls on the Qualla Indian Reservation

Mingo Falls ★

Stream: Mingo Creek	USGS Quad: Smokemont, NC
Rating: spectacular	Landowner: Qualla Indian Reservation
Type: cascade and free-fall	Trail length: 250 yards (one way)
Height: 150 feet	Difficulty: moderate (steps)
Stream flow: medium	Elevation: approx. 2,560 feet

Directions to the trailhead

Start at the intersection of U.S. 441 (Newfound Gap Road) and the Blue Ridge Parkway just inside the southern boundary of the park. Drive south toward Cherokee for 0.5 mile and turn left onto Saunooke Bridge Road. Proceed 0.1 mile to an intersection and turn left onto Big Cove Road. Proceed 4.6 miles and turn right into Mingo Falls campground. Proceed straight ahead into the parking area.

the beautiful lower cascades of Mingo Falls

Trail and description

      Mingo Falls is in my opinion one of the most beautiful waterfalls in the Smokies. Of course the waterfall is actually on the Qualla Indian Reservation and not inside the national park. It's convenient to Cherokee, it's a short walk, and it's just too gorgeous to miss.

      Follow the trail that leads from the parking area up a series of about 160 steps. The trail then levels and heads up to a footbridge over Mingo Creek about 30 yards downstream of the waterfall. Mingo Falls is a near perfect combination of free-falls and steep cascades. A steep scramble path leads to the top of the waterfall and beyond, but do not attempt this. The rocks at the top of the waterfall are very dangerous and the view is perfect from the base. Enjoy the beauty of Mingo Falls from the safety of the footbridge. Note: be sure to be on good behavior as you are guest on the Qualla Indian Reservation.

Soco Falls

Stream: Soco Creek   USGS Quad: Sylva North, NC
Rating: excellent   Landowner: Qualla Indian Reservation
Type: steep cascade   Trail length: 60 yards (one way)
Height: 35 feet   Difficulty: easy
Stream flow: small   Elevation: approx. 3,840 feet

Directions to the trailhead

      From U.S. 19 and the Blue Ridge Parkway at Soco Gap drive north on U.S. 19 toward Cherokee. Proceed 1.4 miles to the large gravel pull-off on the left. Use caution turning across traffic as the pull-off is in a broad right curve.

Trail and description

      This beautiful waterfall has traditionally been a place where visitors left so much trash that you just really did not want to linger here. However on my last visit the trash situation had improved dramatically. A path descends from the pull-off to a recently constructed deck above the brink of this scenic double waterfall. A steep, *dangerous* scramble path descends to the base of this intricate cascade where two separate waterfalls merge to form a common stream - Soco Creek. Best to enjoy this one from the deck as the scramble path passes within a few yards of the dangerous brink of the waterfall.

INDEX

Author's choice for top waterfalls to visit
(distances are one way shortest route)

Northeastern Georgia best of the best ─────────────

Dahlonega hub
• Amicalola Falls	0.25 mile	p 4	moderate

Turner's Corner hub
• Helton Creek Falls	150 yards	p 13	easy

Helen hub
• Anna Ruby Falls	0.4 mile	p 20	moderate
• Dukes Creek Falls	1.1 miles	p 22	moderate
• Raven Cliffs Falls	2.5 miles	p 24	moderate
• Horsetrough Falls	200 yards	p 27	easy
• Blue Hole Falls	1.0 mile	p 29	moderate

Lower Tallulah Basin hub
• Minnehaha Falls	0.3 mile	p 44	easy
• Toccoa Falls	200 yards	p 33	easy
• Panther Creek Falls	3.5 miles	p 34	moderate
• Hurricane Falls	1.0 mile	p 38	easy
• Tempesta Falls	0.8 mile	p 37	easy
• L'Eau d'or Falls	200 yards	p 36	easy
• Hemlock Falls	1.0 mile	p 48	moderate

Northeast Rabun County hub
• Mud Creek Falls	roadside	p 65	easy
• Holcomb Creek Falls	0.5 mile	p 66	moderate
• Martin Creek Falls	0.5 mile	p 61	moderate

Cohutta Wilderness
• Jack's River Falls	4.0 miles	p 72	moderate

Author's choice for top waterfalls to visit
(distances are one way shortest route)

Southwestern North Carolina best of the best ————————————

Highlands - Franklin hub
• Dry Falls	roadside	p 119	easy
• Cullasaja Falls	roadside	p 121	easy
• Glen Falls	0.8 mile	p 123	moderate
• Bridal Veil Falls	roadside	p 118	easy

Cashiers - Sapphire hub
• Whitewater Falls	0.25 mile	p 131	easy
• Rainbow Falls	1.5 miles	p 138	strenuous
• Lower Whitewater Falls	2.0 miles	p 102	moderate
• Silver Run Falls	200 yards	p 128	easy
• Turtleback Falls	1.7 miles	p 141	strenuous
• Schoolhouse Falls	1.2 miles	p 148	moderate
• Greenland Creek Falls	1.0 miles	p 149	moderate

Rosman - Brevard hub
• Looking Glass Falls	roadside	p 159	easy
• Courthouse Falls	0.35 mile	p 157	easy
• Cove Creek Falls	1.25 miles	p 164	moderate
• Lower Falls	0.3	p 166	moderate
• Skinny Dip Falls	0.4 mile	p 165	moderate
• Bubbling Springs Branch	roadside	p 169	easy
• Log Hollow Branch	0.5 mile	p 163	easy

DuPont State Forest - Brevard/Hendersonville
• Triple Falls	0.35 mile	p 174	moderate
• High Falls	1.0 mile	p 175	moderate
• Bridal Veil Falls	2.0 miles	p 176	moderate
• Hooker Falls	0.3 miles	p 173	easy

Other notable falls
• Pearson's Falls	0.3 mile	p 180	easy
• Hickory Nut Falls	0.7 mile	p 181	moderate
• Crabtree Falls	1.0 mile	p 182	moderate
• Linville Falls	1.0 mile	p 183	moderate

Author's choice for top waterfalls to visit
(distances are one way shortest route)

Northwestern South Carolina best of the best

Long Creek hub
- Falls on Brasstown Creek   0.2 mile   p 80   moderate
- Long Creek Falls   1.6 miles   p 76   moderate

Northwest Oconee County hub
- Yellow Branch Falls   1.5 miles   p 90   moderate
- Lower Whitewater Falls   2.0 miles   p 102   moderate
- King Creek Falls   0.6 mile   p 97   moderate
- Station Cove Falls   0.7 mile   p 99   easy

Pickens and Greenville County hub
- Raven Cliffs Falls   2.2 mile   p 108   moderate
- Twin Falls   0.25 mile   p 105   easy
- Falls Creek Falls   1.4 miles   p 114   strenuous

Great Smoky Mountains National Park best of the best

Elkmont Section - Gatlinburg
- Laurel Falls   1.3 miles   p 186   moderate

LeConte Section - Gatlinburg
- Rainbow Falls   2.7 mile   p 189   strenuous
- Grotto Falls   1.5 miles   p 190   moderate

Greenbrier Section
- Ramsey Cascades   4.0 miles   p 193   strenuous

Cades Cove Section
- Abrams Falls   2.5 miles   p 194   moderate

Deep Creek Section - Bryson City
- Indian Creek Falls   1.0 mile   p 201   moderate

Qualla Reservation - Cherokee
- Indian Creek Falls   250 yards   p 202   moderate

Author's choice - top SHORT HIKES to waterfalls in this guide
(best for children, seniors, or if you're in a big hurry!)

Northeast Georgia
- Anna Ruby Falls   p 20
- Minnehaha Falls   p 44
- Toccoa Falls   p 33
- Helton Creek Falls   p 13
- Horsetrough Falls   p 27
- Trahlyta Falls   p 12
- Tempesta Falls   p 37
- Hurricane Falls   p 38
- L'eau d'or Falls   p 36
- Desoto Falls   p 10

The Great Smoky Mountains
- Mingo Falls   p 202
- Laurel Falls   p 186
- Indian Creek Falls   p 201
- Juneywhank Falls   p 199
- Tom's Branch Falls   p 200
- Grotto Falls   p 190

Northwestern South Carolina
- Twin Falls   p 105
- King Creek Falls   p 97
- Issaqueena Falls   p 88
- Yellow Branch Falls   p 90
- Station Cove Falls   p 99
- Wildcat Falls   p 110
- Pig Pen Falls   p 94
- Spoonauger Falls   p 98
- Reedy Branch Falls   p 79

Southwest North Carolina
- Whitewater Falls   p 131
- Dry Falls   p 119
- Silver Run Falls   p 128
- Triple Falls   p 174
- High Falls (Little River) p 175
- Looking Glass Falls   p 159
- Big Laurel Falls   p 125
- Pearson's Falls   p 180
- Linville Falls   p 183
- Hickory Nut Falls   p 181

The dirty dozen (+1) - my most challenging waterfall hikes
hikes to avoid at all cost if you're out of shape or have small kids!

- **Ramsey Cascades** - Great Smoky Mountains National Park, TN
  8 miles round trip - 2,000 ft. elevation change - p 193

- **Rainbow Falls** - Great Smoky Mountains National Park, TN
  5.4 miles round trip - 1,700 ft. elevation change - p 189

- **Raven Cliffs Falls** - Mountain Bridge Wilderness, SC
  8.5 mile loop* - 1,200 foot elevation change - p 108
  (* there is an easier and shorter alternate hike)

- **Laurel Fork Falls** - Foothills Trail, SC
  16+ miles round trip - long, tiring hike - p 104

- **Falls Creek Falls** - Mountain Bridge Wilderness, SC
  2.8 miles round trip - 1,000 foot elevation gain - p 114

- **Bridal Veil Falls** - Tallulah Gorge State Park, GA
  2 miles round trip - approx. 600 foot elevation gain - p 41

- **Lower Falls on Fall Creek** - Sumter National Forest, SC
  4 miles round trip - no real path, elevation change - p 85

- **Jack's River Falls** - Cohutta Wilderness, GA
  8.0 miles round trip - 500 foot elevation change - p 72

- **Singley's Falls** - Overflow Creek, GA
  6.4 miles round trip - approx. 700 foot elevation gain - p 69

- **Rainbow Falls** - Horsepasture River, NC
  3.0 miles round trip - approx. 700 ft. elevation change - p 128

- **Rainbow Falls** - YMCA Camp Greenville, SC
  1 mile round trip - approx. 400 foot elevation change - p 112

- **Opossum Creek Falls** - Sumter National Forest, SC
  5.0 miles round trip - approx. 500 foot elevation change - p 78

- **Blue Hole Falls** - Sumter National Forest, SC
  1 mile round trip - tricky stream crossing followed by a
  nerve-racking descent along a dangerous path - p 91

note that there are three "Rainbow Falls" on the list...

Recommended resources to expand your waterfall library

- *Waterfalls of North Georgia, Images of North Georgia's Wonders of Nature*
  by John D. Anthony, Jr.; Yahoolavista Publishing, Dahlonega, GA

- *North Carolina Waterfalls, A Hiking and Photography Guide*
  by Kevin Adams; John F. Blair Publishing, Winston-Salem, NC

- *The Waterfalls of South Carolina*
  by Benjamin Brooks and Tim Cook; PCF Press, Columbia, SC
  www.palmettoconservation.org

- *Waterfalls and Cascades of the Great Smoky Mountains*
  by Hal Hubbs, Charles Maynard, David Morris
  Panther Press, Seymour, TN

- *North Carolina Waterfalls, A Hiking and Photography Guide*
  by Kevin Adams; John F. Blair Publishing, Winston-Salem, NC

- *Waterfall Walks and Drives in the Great Smoky Mountains and the Western Carolinas*
  by Mark Morrison; H. F. Publishing, Douglasville, GA

- *Waterfalls of the Blue Ridge: A Guide to the Blue Ridge Parkway and the Great Smoky Mountains National Park*
  by Blouin, Bordonaro, Bordonaro
  Menasha Ridge Press, Birmingham, AL

- *A Guide's Guide to Panthertown Valley* (map)
  by Burt Kornegay; Slickrock Expeditions, Cullowhee, NC

About the author - Brian A. Boyd

A lifelong hiker, avid outdoorsman and amateur photographer, Brian Boyd published his first southern Appalachian guidebook, *The Chattooga Wild and Scenic River,* back in 1990. That same year Brian founded Fern Creek Press as a small, independent publisher of local guidebooks and maps.

In the twenty years since, Boyd has published over fifteen guidebooks describing some of his favorite areas and detailing topics of local historical interest. Some of Boyd's other works include *The North Georgia Mountains Pocket Companion, The Highlands-Cashiers Outdoors Companion, Boyd's Guide to Georgia's Rabun County, Yesterday's Rabun, Summits of the South, The Great Smoky Mountains Pocket Companion, The Tallulah Falls Railroad - A Photographic Remembrance,* and *Secrets of Tallulah.*

The mission of Fern Creek Press is to publish easy-to-use niche guides that explore the southern Appalachian region. Some of these books detail subjects that normally would not attract big-name publishers. Boyd's simple straight-forward narratives contain concise, accurate information in an easy-to-use format and at a reasonable price. What you may not know is that Boyd personally handles the entire project including writing, photography, maps, layout and the distribution of his publications as well.

Boyd is currently employed full-time in communications and public relations at Tallulah Falls School, a private college preparatory school near his home. In his spare time he continues to explore the southern Appalachian region and write and publish new projects. Brian and his wife, Kay, currently live in Clarkesville. They have three grown children.

Boyd enjoys speaking to church or civic groups about his passion for the natural wonders and history of the region. He can be reached at 706.982.3635.

John 3:16 • Proverbs 3:5-6

Notes

Notes